Estrangement

Deanna Cooner PhD

Estrangement

Copyright © 2020 by Deanna Cooner, All rights reserved

Unless otherwise indicated all Scripture quotations are from the Holy Bible, New American Standard Version, 1995 by Lockman Foundation; A Corporation Not for profit, La Habra, Ca. All rights reserved.

No part of this publication may be reproduced, stored in a retrieval system or transmitted in any way to any means, electronic, mechanical, photocopy, recording or otherwise without the prior permission of the author except as provided by USA copyright law.

The opinions expressed by the author are not necessarily those of Stones In Clay Publishing.

Stones in Clay Publishing

P.O. Box 1302

Newcastle, Ok 73065

Living stones, being built up as a spiritual house for a holy priesthood, to offer up spiritual sacrifices acceptable to God through Jesus Christ. 1 Peter 2:5,

But we have this treasure in jars of clay, to show that the surpassing power belongs to God and not to us. 2 Corinthians 4:7

Cover Art by Katherine Holmes Booth

Cover Design and Graphics by Gary Cooner

Published in United States of America

ISBN: 978-1-7337093-4-7
Family /Spiritual Growth / Christian / General
2020.02.15

Stones in Clay
PUBLISHING

Contents

1 Upsetting Normal 1
   Trauma Upsets All That Is Normal 8
   The Pain 8
   What Happened? 12

2 The Plot 17
   Exchanging Family For Culture 21
   Discipline Is Teaching 19
   When Estrangement Begins 21
   The Family 25
   The Deeds of the Flesh 30

3 Reasons 35
   Who and What Are These Gods? 36
   Modern Gods 41
   The Hidden Gods 42
   Sexual Deviation 46
   Grumbling 46
   Timing 48
   History 50

4 Demons 52
   Sacrifice to Demons 55
   Self-Esteem and Estrangement 59
   Warning 65

5 God's Plan 67
   The Beginning 68
   Worship of The Serpent 72
   Restoring The Family 75

6 God's Image 83
Why Did God Regret Creating Man? 84
Starting Over? 86
Why Doubt? 89
7 The Schemes Of The Serpent 91
Confusion 93
Buzz Words 97
Emotional Abuse 98
Narcissistic 99
Gaslighting 103
Toxic 104
No-Contact 105
Stonewalling 112
You Ruined My Life 114
Reaction to Buzz Words 115
The Problem! 116
8 New Age Influence 118
The Church Problem 124
New Age-Cause of Estrangement? 129
9 Contending 134
The Fight Begins 135
The Prodigal Child 140
10 The Weeping Prophet 142
The New Covenant 147
The Old Covenant-Mosaic Covenant 149
To Whom Is the New Covenant Given? 155
Interpretation of New Covenant 162
11 A Tragic Story, A Happy Ending 167
The Rest of the Story 171

Summation 173
    For The Estranged Parent of an Adult Child 173
    Notes for the Estranged Adult Child 174
End Notes 177

1
Upsetting Normal

I COULD HEAR it in her voice. My daughter was injured. Not physically but spiritually. Her mournful cry "Mamas don't leave, painted a picture of her pain which reached beyond words.

I took a firm stand and reminded her, "you're not her mama, you're her friend."

My daughter's close friend shared her many life struggles with my daughter. Nonetheless, she connected with the friend and her family and so did I. With a gentle helping heart, my daughter was often pulled into the friend's latest crisis. I helped my daughter solve some of the friend's problem by providing equipment, transportation, meals, and time whatever was needed to solve the friend's crisis. Not because I liked the friend, rather because I loved my daughter.

During one of the more serious crisis with this friend my daughter felt deep emotional upset over her inability to help her friend. The friend's problem reached into my daughter's life and created a crisis for her.

My daughter was wounded and I didn't understand the depth of her wound. This time I offered no solace or support. I reasoned my daughter was tired and would be herself once she had a good night's rest.

Trauma Upsets All That Is Normal

The trauma in a person's life causes the flight, fight or freeze response. Fright entered the heart and brain of my sweet helpful daughter. She called me for needed affirmation. Instead, I told her she wasn't the friend's mother, in a rather harsh tone.

I met her a few days later. She was talking about the nurse and was visibly upset. I tried to remain calm by listening and changing the subject. Mistake number two, she needed to talk, to rant, to get rid of her fear. I ignored her pain and her fear.

She informed me she would not be seeing me the next day at our planned activity. She was going home. I felt she would be better when she had a good night's sleep. She had driven ten hours to be with me. Surely she wouldn't make the ten-hour trip back the next morning. As we parted, she climbed into her car and looked back at me. I thought to myself. *That's not my daughter.*

Now two years later, she only speaks to me when necessary and usually with a hostile tone. Those rare conversations have dwindled to nothing. She will not speak to me at all. She is estranged from me.

The Pain

C.S. Lewis wrote two books concerning grieving, the first he wrote before he experienced the death of a loved one, *The Problem of Pain* written in 1940. The second book he wrote after his wife, Joy, died of cancer, *A Grief Observed* written in 1960. This text is the after for me, although it is not about my situation, there is an understanding in it that comes from the pain of estrangement. The text you hold in your hand is **not** my story. I don't need to share my story because if you are reading this, you have your own story and your own pain. This text is the story of the One who gives hope and endured through the pain. It is the story of a Father who is estranged from His children and how He made a way for them to be reconciled to Him. It is the hope given in Jesus Christ.

The problem of estrangement is wide-spread and growing, especially among active church-going Christian families. I'm not presenting any statistics to back this up, nor will I search for them, because statistics don't matter if it is happening in one's family, that one statistic is enough. The more important point is why? Why is this happening in Christian homes with people who know the peace of Christ? It should not be happening in the Christian family? That question haunted me while I cried out to God in my pain. I lay awake at night trying to come up with a plan to "fix it." I kept quiet not sharing my pain with anyone. When people asked me about my daughter I put on a brave smile and said they were doing great. I didn't know if it was true or not, for I have been shut out of their life. The worst part of the whole ordeal came with the realization, I didn't know why and she wouldn't tell me specifics but instead made generalizations regarding my personality, even accusing me of put-downs and insults. This accusation is one of perception. As her mother, my desire is to build-up and encourage my child.

I write this with an understanding heart. Jesus wrote His understanding in the shedding of His blood to reconcile the children to the Father. Therefore, our hope and peace lie in the words written by our Father to us, His children.

Whether you are the person who has been abandoned by your family or the one that has left the family unit, there is hope and a promise in Malachi 4:6, "He will turn the hearts of the fathers to the children and the hearts of the children toward the fathers."

This promise is the last prophecy given in the Old Testament. The primary prophecy given by the Old Testament prophets regarded the coming of Jesus Christ and His ministry. Luke refers to this passage when the birth of John is announced as the predecessor to Jesus ministry. John's preaching will "turn many of the sons of Israel back to the Lord their God." So there will no longer be a curse or a ban upon Israel.

Malachi 4:5 announces the time of the fulfillment of the prophecy to be the "great and terrible day of the Lord." Luke 1:17 refers to the prophecy; *"It is he who will go as a forerunner before Him in the spirit and power of Elijah, to turn the hearts of the fathers back to the children, and the disobedient to the attitude of the righteous, so as to make ready a people prepared for the Lord."*

Luke refers to the prophecy in Malachi as an illustration of John the Baptist being a forerunner to Christ's ministry. Malachi announces the time of the fulfillment of the prophecy to be the "great and terrible day of the Lord." The message appears to be one like Elijah will escort Jesus second coming in the same way John the Baptist escorted Jesus ministry on earth.

When Jesus returns, one like Elijah will announce His return and His preaching will restore families through judgment. Since God wants a family, His children must understand the nature of His family.

The first time Jesus came to restore God's children, it was through teaching, love, grace and taking the punishment of the curse or the ban, the separation from God. When He returns the curse will be removed through the judgment. Either one seeks and finds the grace of Christ's sacrifice for them, or they reject it.

This grace cannot be seen unless one is restored to the family unit. One cannot understand the sacrifice nor the love of grace, if they cannot see beyond hurt feelings and disputes to see the heart of God beating in their earthly family. Therefore, it appears Elijah's preaching or teaching will allow the estranged to see the need for restoration in their family as an illustration of the need for reconciliation into the family of God.

This prophecy does not promise that all families will be healed during their journey on earth. It does promise all those who know Jesus in a personal relationship will be restored so that the curse of estrangement will not reside in the hearts of God's people as they enter into His family. In other words, whatever, the reason you have cut off your family whether it be parent, child or sibling, it will be resolved by those who belong to God to give the family a pure heart.

If there is a promise of a solution, then there is a problem. He knew this was going to happen, and He gave the broken-hearted estranged parents, and children hope. This is not a surprise to God, but it is an event that teaches us about God's heart and His eternal plan. Pain is a terrible teacher, but a good one.

What Happened?

It comes as a surprise. It is seldom planned by either side, it just happens. Or so it seems. The incident that appears to be the causation is often minor, not great enough to cause a disturbance between family members. The shock of being abandoned is the same as the shock of a sudden death of a family member. The process of trying to understand takes on a life of its own.[1]

A parent is most often the one estranged by an adult child. When it occurs, shock is often followed by denial. The estranged parent thinks it will pass. It is so far removed from the personality of the family unit; it can't be real. The next step is formed in statements such as, "You crossed the line and you ruined my life." The statements help the estranged to realize the seriousness of the event and it gives weaponry to the estranger.

The next stage is reliving every moment and every word looking for the offense that caused such a devastating blow. Lying awake at night and repeating every word, studying every nuance etc. Spending the days creating conversations of apology, followed by a conversation of explanation and finally a conversation of rebuke, only to start over on the imaginary conversations again. Then comes the anger, the need to explode. The need to have someone understand and make it better. The need for someone to explain it.

The adult child needs to share their story of their hurt to friends or family or anyone who will listen, while the estranged parent melts into a pool of shame after the friends of the adult child refuse to speak to them. The estranged parent feels the anger of the child expressed through those friends of the adult child. The parent is shut out of the conversation. The adult child has shut out the family heritage and life, not only for themselves but for their children.

Soon neither parent or child will speak of it to anyone. While the parent may not know why a loving family member abandoned the family, the adult child builds his case based on the memories formed in childhood. Either party may cry to a few people who happen to be nearby when the pain is the most intense. It is like groaning when the body is hurt. The pain is so fierce one groans and those nearby who see or hear the groan will offer sympathy. Afterward, the estranged regrets speaking of it. The adult child will not talk to their family member upon whom they have cast their anger. The parent asks, "Do they not feel any pain?" The answer is yes, both sides feel the pain of estrangement.

The silence of the parent or the justification by the adult child causes shame. Now the ruminating goes beyond the event of the estrangement and into childhood and young adulthood memories. For the parent, they search for a reason, for the adult child seeks justification for their action.

The simplest statement by the estranged parent or adult child seeking a reconciliation sets the one separating from the family into a frenzy leading to chastisement of the other. This leads to a complete decimation of the estranged family member. The evisceration by the departing family member silences the estranged family members, even siblings and extended family avoid the gross bleeding wound in the family unit. The family is broken and all members feel there is no recourse for reconciliation. Hopelessness and self-loathing replaces hope. When there is conversation and attempts to mend the rift in the family, words of denigration are used against the family members. Words such as narcissistic, a mental disorder which is used to attack the estranged family. The descriptions are frightening to both parties and the family members on the fringe because once the words are used as an accusation against a once-beloved family member the anger is justified and it turns into a need for vengeance for the perceived wrongs they have suffered.

All this and **Nothing happened!** This cannot be emphasized enough. Most family estrangements happen over nothing more than perceived wrongs. Even if there was a legitimate disagreement, it is never enough to abandon a family. The ideas become unreasonable and turned into a weapon to injure the other party who they perceive committed wrongs against them. It now passes into unreasonableness and the more the one who feels they were injured by the other the greater their desire to inflict pain. Thus the estrangement becomes the weapon to gain justice. The more they hurt the perceived guilty party, the more the victim desires to hurt them. Extreme measures are now employed. This allows the victim to deal with their pain. Yes, the one who does the estranging will feel the pain of loss. It will be different and not as visible, but present.

For the one left a flood of tears erupts. It is like a breaking dam, it can't be stopped. It goes for hours, then days, then weeks. Then exhaustion and emotional emptiness create a point where the crying stops as suddenly as it started. The next phase is total resignation of the one that has been estranged, to their own awfulness and evilness. At this point suicidal or death thoughts cloud the mind of the estranged for there is no other escape from the pain. Death is the only solution. The estranged who does not know the reasons for the estrangement will find it easy to blame themselves.

The resignation is not acceptance or the ability to move forward with life. It is the result of exhaustion. Acceptance is a daily ritual which eventually becomes easier, until one day, the estranged spends a whole day without thinking about the one who abandoned them. That is the beginning of acceptance.

What is happening? Now it's time to get down and find some answers. Where does a broken heart start to find mending? The church of course. Nonetheless, material produced by the Christian community comes up short. Most of the research done on the topic has been done by secular professionals or written by those suffering from estrangement. More is written from the estranged parental side. This is most likely due to the writing about it being a release of their pain and a chance to tell their side of the story. It can also be attributed to an adult child has their own family and they have moved past the need for parents and focus on their own children and grandchildren.

There are one-sided studies from the viewpoint of the estranger, concluding there is no other way "to heal" except to separate from the family. There is little written about reconciliation efforts because there are few happy endings of reconciliation. The general consensus concludes the abandoned family member must apologize to the one who exiled them. Then there might be some reconciliation. Maybe!

A review of the Christian viewpoint regarding family estrangement turned up some sweet talk about letting go of adult children by letting them learn and respecting their privacy. Once again the church and the Christian community is missing a need and a growing problem. A problem that is insidious in its planned outcome.

This is not a happen stance, this is a cleverly designed attack of the enemy against God's plan, the church and the family. If the church has no answer and is also a victim, the next place to look is in scripture; God's holy word. Does the Bible address the problem of family estrangement? The answer is a resounding yes, repairing family estrangement is basically the theme of the entire Bible. God is the heavenly father, building an eternal family by repairing the estrangement of His children.

2
The Plot

LET'S TAKE A look at the biblical history of mankind and his relationship to God the Father.

Genesis 3 begins the downfall of mankind when the "clever" or "crafty" serpent approached the woman and asked her a simple question. *"You mean God put all these beautiful trees in the garden and then told you not to eat any of their fruit."*

Do you see the cleverness of the lie? The serpent is questioning God's integrity. The woman answered with the words of God, *"No, he said don't eat of the tree in the center of the garden or you will surely die."*

The clever serpent sets the stage for the next two lies rolled together in one sentence. *"Surely, you won't die, He knows if you eat of the tree you will be like gods."*

When the serpent presents this argument; *the woman **looks** at the fruit, **sees** it is good for food, and then **takes** it.* This three-step process of falling for the enemy's deception has not changed. It is the same method used against Christian families to devour future generations. (Ephesians 2:2-3)

This plot seeks destruction of the image of God and His family. Remember when the people told Samuel, they wanted a king to rule over them. *The Lord said to Samuel, "Listen to the voice of the people in regard to all that they say to you, for they have not rejected you, but they have rejected Me from being king over them. I Samuel 8:7*

The people had good reason to reject Samuel since he appointed his worthless and greedy sons to follow him. They would easily succumb to bribes and empty promises rather than practice the justice of God. When God says the people are rejecting Him, it means the people do not trust Him as much as they fear the worthless judges.

While the physical world presented a plausible reason, the truth behind the request was to change their government from a theocracy to a monarchy. Why would they want to do this? The plot is the clever work of the serpent to replace a man after God's own heart with a leader after the serpent's heart; a heart filled with pride. (Isaiah 14:13-14)

The people reasoned a king would take care of them and fight their battles for them. God instructed Samuel to warn the people about what would happen if they served a king instead of their God. Samuel did, and laid it out pretty clear about the downside. (I Samuel 8:10-22). Still they wanted a king.

This should be sounding a bit familiar. Look at John 8:44-45. Jesus tells the people Satan is a murderer and a liar, and then He says, *"I tell you the truth, but you will not believe me."*

The plot of the enemy is simple, teach a believable lie. This concept appears to be a bit ridiculous. However, the philosopher Immanuel Kant, built a popular idea known as the 'Lie for the Common Good.' A treatise on the ethics of lying which is still studied as the 'Categorical Imperative." [2] in colleges today. The simple basic of the philosophy states that, 'if you're going to tell a lie, make it believable, otherwise you will be seen as a fool.' The serpent is most clever in this area. He is the father of lies and knows how to make them believable.

Parental estrangement is a believable lie built by the father of lies for the purpose of destroying God's people and making their testimonies impotent. It is the lie designed to denigrate God's picture of eternity in the kingdom of God, found in the biblical family unit. This is the plot, but how is it accomplished? And how does one restore their family unit?

Discipline Is Teaching

The disciplining methods used by parents to address the problems of childhood, teen years and young adult set the stage for the for adult child. The methods vary with each family. This illustrates the need for the church to provide biblically based parenting skills for the congregation. Deuteronomy 6:6 is Moses telling the people how to parent their children when they enter the Promised land. He says, "teach them diligently." Teach them the laws of God, talk about them when you rise up and when you sit down, when you walk, write them upon the doorposts of your home. In other words, raise children in the Word of God.

However, abusive punishment is never in God's plan. This text addresses families who disciplined with teaching. Punishment would be administered for defiance of a parent's rule for teaching life lessons.

When an imperfect human disciplines through their ideas which are not biblical, it can create problems for the adult child. The extreme cases allow opportunity for both parent and child to understand God's plan of forgiveness. (1 Peter 4:12-19)

Jesus knows the pain of these situations and He feels every blow and attack. He weeps for those suffering as well as those applying physical hurt to another. Yet, even while on the cross Jesus said, "Forgive them, for they know not what they do." Humans carry that hurt they endured as children deep in their spirits and they need love and help. Part of that help may be to have little contact with the abusive parent, but they should be able to respond in the short term if a parent calls. In other words, completely cutting a parent or a child out of the other's life will not bring about any healing. It just pushes it aside. When healing occurs there will probably not be a joyful reunion and a happy family result, but there will be peace. The abuser that does not change will move on without the pain of loss. The one abused will be able to move on with peace because they didn't disobey the commandment to 'honor father and mother' or the instructions found in the aforementioned passage in 1 Peter with emphasis on 1 Peter 4:11.

The child who gives honor to an abusive parent serves as a testimony to that parent of the forgiving grace of Christ. That may be the only picture they see of Christ's truth, love and forgiveness.

> *"Whoever speaks, is to do so as one who is speaking the utterances of God: whoever serves to do so as one who is serving by the strength, which God supplies; so that in all things God may be glorified through Jesus Christ to whom belongs the glory and dominion forever and ever. Amen."* (1 Peter 4:11).

It's about Christ, not a parent or an adult child that is wounded, it is about Christ who was wounded for our transgressions. The penalty of an abusive parent or a disrespectful child has already been paid. Rejoice in the suffering so that Christ may be glorified. (1 Peter 4:13).

Exchanging Family for Culture

> *Has a nation changed gods when they were not gods? But My people have changed their glory for that which does not profit. Jeremiah 2:11*

> *This is what the Lord says; What fault did your ancestors find in me, that they strayed so far from me? They followed worthless idols and became worthless themselves. Jeremiah 2:5 (NIV)*

The event which causes an adult child to leave a parent is a turning point for them and devastation for the parent. It has been described as worse than the death of a child. It is difficult for an estranged parent to express this sentiment because it sounds heartless. In truth, neither event is easy, but the parent of the deceased child knows a conclusion, maybe even a cause or a reason. They have a platform on which to stand. When one buries a beloved family member, they are left with happy memories and a family member that never withdrew love from the family. The estranged parent seldom has anything upon which to stand except the cryptic words used against them by their adult child.

The act of estrangement is a spiritual death for both parties. Yet it is seldom treated as a spiritual event. Most often the professionals will look for the failure of the parent in their parenting skills. For the adult child separating from their aging parents, they will be told they "need to heal" from their raising, or maybe it comes from a collective thinking of a me generation that regards anything in life that is troublesome should be expunged in order to be "happy."

In reality all families are dysfunctional because they are made up of imperfect humans. (Romans 3:12). Even with extensive training and church seminars, parents are still left to address situations unique to each child and unique to the family. Children are the perfect example of the spiritual state of adults without Christ. Parents provide unconditional love to a child to illustrate the unconditional love of a perfect Lord. However, parents are often the image of the wrath of God found in the Old Testament.

Without Old Testament teaching in the home and church, the child does not recognize that wrath can show the ultimate love. A parent attempting to raise their children in accordance to the righteousness of God will express wrath at those things which cause harm to their child. A child who trusts the parents will save themselves a lot of heart ache. Even adult children need to trust their Christian parents. They can disagree and maybe even know better, but the trust of their unconditional love should never be questioned. Just as we cannot question the love of Christ for us, but we often question the path He leads. Human parents are not perfect in their methods; they are perfect in their love. An adult child who cannot accept this will rob themselves and their children of much needed guidance given in love while navigating through a dark and heartless world.

When Estrangement Begins

When one estranges from the family unit or from a family member, a rumbling of strange feelings shocks the family. The beloved child or sibling or even a parent suddenly change into someone and something totally different. The once intact family finds they have been invaded by a hateful, resentful, rebellious, unreasonable, unforgiving, angry person. A person who physically looks like their beloved family member and is remembered as a loving sensitive person now causing strife and division. All the things Paul mentions in Galatians 5:20, the deeds of the flesh are evident and the family experiences them firsthand.

Recognizing the status of one or both parties involved in a family estrangement as a believer and follower of Christ sets the problem within a spiritual scope. Nonetheless, even the non-believing family is vulnerable to the schemes of a spiritual enemy known as the father of lies.

Many estrangements are built on a foundation of perceived wrongs rather than an understanding of actual events. There are times a party has been injured by life events and these events are transferred to the family members. "There is significant evidence of interpersonal rejection or exclusion can trigger physiological changes in the brain that are similar to those experienced by a physical threat."[3]

The event which triggers the estrangement can be interpreted by the brain as an actual physical danger transferring the threat to a family member as the source of the danger.

To illustrate; when Chelsea met with her mother after a particular harrowing ordeal, she needed to release the anxiety of the previous experience. Her mother thought her anxious behavior was a result of being tired. Mom, listened to her explosive comments about the incident but didn't console or confirm her actions. As a result, Chelsea felt her mother didn't care and the brain perceived the mother's reaction as unloving and the cause of the danger.

In the following days, Chelsea felt her feeling were unimportant to her mother. At that point her mother's personality served Chelsea as the source of injury. Soon she pulled away from her mother. When she did speak to her, the anger she felt at the previous experience brought on scathing reprimand from Chelsea. Her brain interpreted her mother as the cause of the anxiety.

While there are studies confirming this phenomenon, biblical evidence of a spiritual interference can be found in Galatians 3:1-5.[4] The spiritual influence promotes the destruction of the family model God designed and gave to His children.

This evil spiritual element is not benign. It produces a rift in the family built on the perception it plants in the mind rather than facts. The perception felt is pain. "Pain exists when neural circuits conclude that danger exists and that action is required."[5]

When trauma occurs, the person nearest the one traumatized is interpreted by the brain as the cause of the trauma or pain. "At this point the brain demands one stop and prevent the damage in the body, this action will change one's behavior."[6]

Before the Babylonians completely took over Jerusalem, God gave His children instructions to live in the foreign land. They have experienced trauma and will see more of it. God is giving them instructions to overcome the trauma without fear. Let's look at the instructions and the pattern God give His children.

The Family

Jeremiah 29:11 is one of the most oft quoted scriptures. It says,

"For, I know the plans I have for you, plans for good not evil to give you a future and a hope."

The wall décor usually stops there, but there is actually more to the concept in the surrounding verses.

"For." The first word in this promise refers to the conditions mentioned before the promise. This means there are some conditions that must be honored first. God gives instructions that appear to be the opposite the people's expectations.

- *Build houses and live in them, plant gardens and eat their produce. Jeremiah 29:5.* This first condition addresses one's physical needs, shelter and food. These are the things which parents lovingly provided to the child from birth to the point of building their own home and raising food. God as the heavenly Father tells His Children He will provide in this foreign land. The estranged family must trust the provision of God for their needs even though they are entering foreign territory. An angry family member trashes the family leaving them vulnerable and lost. This verse establishes the family member's physical needs in this different and unwanted territory. Don't stop living. Taking this a step further than the physical needs, God addresses the next stage of life.

- *Take wives and become the father of sons and daughters., take wives for your sons and give your daughters to husbands, that they may bear sons and daughters, and multiply these and do not decrease. Jeremiah 29:6.* God wants us to build a family. This passage is talking to the Israelites as they are watching the Babylonians outside the city gates preparing to sack their city. This is God's instructions? The city is about to be pillaged and burned but God is telling them to build houses, plant gardens, plan weddings and have children. It doesn't fit. God is preparing them for a future living with Babylonians in Babylon. It is going to happen and nothing will stop it at this point, so God prepares His children to succeed and overcome the trauma. The estranged family is to build a life and a family in spite of their loss. It isn't the answer they want or need. It is ridiculous. God must be taking a nap. What they want and need is for the Military Calvary to arrive and defeat the Babylonians and let them continue to live their blissful life of ignorance in Jerusalem. When the trauma is interpreted in the limited knowledge of the one experiencing the trauma, the traumatic moment becomes the pivot of life and the one with them becomes the instigator of that trauma.

- *Seek the welfare of the city where I have sent you into exile, and pray to the Lord on its behalf; for in its welfare you will have welfare. Jeremiah 29:7.* What! God wants me to pray for my enemy? Is He asking an estranged parent or child to pray for the welfare of a rebellious child or selfish parent? Yes, He is. He told the Israelites to pray for Babylon and to ask for all of God's benefits upon the city of their enemies. The enemies that are raping, killing, starving, beating, burning and stealing the treasures of the temple are the very people for whom God instructs His people to pray. Pray for that family member that is ravishing the family unit.

- *"Do not let your prophets who are in your midst and your diviners deceive you, and do not listen to the dreams which they dream." Jeremiah 29:8.* Who are the prophets among an estranged family? Anyone giving advise contrary to God's word and plan. This can be those causing the traumatic event or those interpreting the events such as counselors, pastors, teachers, friends and other family. When one discloses their hurt at being estranged or their hurt which caused them to estrange from their family, they are setting themselves up as a victim. It is the nature of natural man to seek retribution and vengeance from those who injure us. Yet, this is the very thing God instructs His people NOT to do. Therefore, do not listen to anyone speaking contrary to God's will and plan. *"For they prophecy falsely and I have not sent them." Declares the LORD." Jeremiah 29:10.* A seventy-year exile does occur for God's children, but it is not from Him, it is for the land He gave them. A family exile will result in lost benefits and support. It may be necessary for the exile to occur in order to recognize the relationship is more important than one's hurt feelings, or loss of control. The rift may change false perceptions into facts.

A glimmer of hope sparkles in the next verse. *"For thus says the LORD, when seventy years have been completed for Babylon, I will visit you and fulfill My good word to you, to bring you back to this place. Jeremiah 29:10.* He will bring His people back to this place, which is their home. A problem is seen in the phrase, "in seventy years." In other words, there will be a time the family will be estranged and that time will be set by God, not by the family wanting to heal the rift. There will be a reason for the time and it will give justice to the one who has estranged from the family as well as peace to the one who has been estranged. God told His children in Leviticus 26:43-44 to give the land its Sabbath by allowing the land to lay fallow (no crops) every seventh year. The people did not do it for 490 years. That meant there were seventy years the land should have not been used. God sent them off the land for seventy years to make up for those Sabbaths that were never observed and to give the land it's rest.[7] The rules of living in the land were precise and since the people didn't obey, God would bring about His statues by providence. A family estrangement may occur because of stringent, lax or unfair rules, either in the past or the present.

A famous verse, Jeremiah 29:11, reveals why, they are to do the things God has asked of them. "Because He knows the plans He has for them, plans for good not evil." But the prior conditions must be met.

This account can be baffling since the commandments God gave His children were in the midst of a calamity. Their city, homes and jobs are ravished and destroyed. God give instructions to build new homes and make families in their land of exile. King Zedekiah disobeyed these rules and as a result his family was slain before his eyes and then he was blinded by Nebuchadnezzar. He lived out his days in a Babylonian jail. It is serious matter to disregard the instructions of God.

In the same way God instructed His children before the Babylonian captivity to help them through the trauma with little damage, so it is with the instructions given to the estranged parent or child who becomes the source of damage to the one traumatized.

It is interesting to note, that most all psychologists who have dealt professionally with the problem of estrangement instruct their counselees, to build a life for themselves. The theory is that no one will want to rejoin a sorrowful, self-pitying person giving up on life. But a healthy relationship can be restored between healthy people.[8]

The final look at this passage comes after the famous verse regarding the plans of God. It has the keyword, "then." If the people build new houses and families in the land of their exile, and trust God has plans for good for them, 'THEN!' *"You will call upon Me and come and pray to Me, and I will listen to you." Jeremiah 29:12.* This is a greater promise than verse eleven. If we follow God's instructions, He will listen to the cries of our heart. Not only does He listen but He answers.

We often get the impression God hears every request we make and this is not true. God hears the prayer of a broken and sincere heart. He does not listen to wish lists and grant them. Our prayers present worship and are the spiritual weapons against the evil spiritual powers. Prayer is a healing balm to the one praying as well as the object of one's prayer. The prayers should be in accordance to God's will and given in trust that He will complete His will for our good and our lost family member.

That's a hard concept to swallow when a mother wants to pick up the phone and call her beloved daughter and ask about a recipe, but she has no number to call. Or when a father wants to repair storm damage, but he has no contact with a son who has the skills, strength and tools. Or a terminal illness strikes the family and the estranged member doesn't care. It's the little things of everyday life that eat away at the spirit and make each day of life another disappointment.

Look at verse 13 of Jeremiah 29. *"You will seek Me and find Me when you search for Me with all your heart."* A wonderful promise of finding God. It doesn't say all will be restored like we want it, it says, God's plans will be carried out and in the process of seeking God, the estranged family on both sides will find that peace that passes understanding. (Philippians 4:7) It will be the calm that comes with complete trust in the ultimate power over the universe and power over the heart of the estranged member. *"God can turn the hearts of kings like water."* Proverbs 21:1.

The Deeds of the Flesh

The deeds of the flesh listed by Paul in Galatians 5:19-21 include: immorality, impurity, sensuality; idolatry, sorcery, enmities, strife, jealousy, outbursts of anger, disputes, dissensions, factions, envying, drunkenness, carousing and things like these. This is quite a list. Let's take a look at each one in light of an estranged family.

Immorality –Any sex act outside the bonds of marriage of one man and one woman. If a child saw sexual immorality in the family, including divorce and remarriage, it may cause difficulty for them as an adult. Once an event triggers transference of physical danger to the family member, then that same mechanism will find past deeds that were difficult or traumatic and use them to keep the hostility toward the family member alive. It shows the impact the event had upon the life of the child. Whatever triggers the estrangement may be linked to that point of life. This leaves one unable to cope with the burst of past feelings gushing out of their mind in the form of emotions. Parents and family are the safety net to release those emotions which cannot be explained.

Impurity –Uncleanness. It is the result of immoral living. Romans 1:24 says, *"God gave them up to uncleanness due to the lust of their hearts."* It can be the result of rebellion, *"Given over to iniquity after iniquity,"* Romans 6:19, It can also refer to greed, (Ephesians 4:19). The opposite of uncleanness is holiness, (1 Thessalonians 4:7).

Sensuality –Unbridled passion, outrageous lust. The desires of one's flesh is so strong it causes a failing of the mind causing one to submit to unlawful lusts. (Proverbs 14:30, 1 Corinthians 7:9)

Idolatry – the worship of other gods and the vices that come from that worship. (1 Samuel 15:23)

Sorcery or witchcraft – magic arts often found in conjunction with idolatry. Isaiah 47:9 reveals the high cost of witchcraft.

Enmities – plain and simple this is hatred and the by-product of it is loss of relationship with God. This is the end emotion which prevents reconciliation. *Romans 8:7, For the mind set on the flesh is death, but the mind set on the Spirit is life and peace, because the mind set on the flesh is hostile toward God, for it does not subject itself to the law of God, for it is not able to do so.*

Strife – a quarrel, strife, divisions. *1 Corinthians 3:2-3, I had to feed you with milk not with solid food, because you weren't ready for anything stronger. And you still aren't ready, for you are still controlled by your sinful nature. You are jealous of one another and quarrel with each other. Doesn't that prove you are controlled by your sinful nature? Aren't you living like people of the world? (NLT)*

Jealousy – a fervor of spirit in defending anything. An indignation, punitive of mind and excitement of the mind. James 3:14, *but if you are bitterly jealous and there is selfish ambition in your heart, don't cover up the truth with boasting and lying. For jealousy and selfishness are not God's kind of wisdom. Such things are earthly, unspiritual, and demonic, for wherever there is jealousy and selfish ambition, there you will find disorder and evil of every kind.*

Outbursts of anger – passion, angry heat boiling from inside and bursting forth, *Luke 4:28, All those in the synagogue became angry when they heard these things.* This occurred when Jesus read from Isaiah and declared that He was the Messiah to fulfill that prophecy. When the truth does not line up with the expectations, anger often develops. Even against the one speaking truth and coming as an act of love.

Disputes – The act of putting oneself in front and declaring partisan ideas creating a factious spirit. Dividing to conquer. James 3:16, for where envying and strife is there is confusion and every evil work.

Dissensions –division, *Romans 16:17-18, Now I urge you, brethren, not those who cause divisions and offenses, contrary to the doctrine which you learned, and avoid* *them. For those who are such do not serve our Lord Jesus Christ, but their own belly, and by smooth words and flattering speech deceive the hearts of the simple.*

Factions – A group following their own sensibilities and taking others captive either by idea or force. *2 Peter 2:1 -3, "But there were also false prophets among the people, even as there will be false teachers among you, who will secretly bring in destructive heresies, even denying the LORD who bought them and bring on themselves swift destruction. And many will follow their destructive ways, because of whom the way of truth will be blasphemed. By covetousness they will exploit you with deceptive words; for a long time, their judgment has not been idle, and their destruction does not slumber."*

Envying – akin to jealousy. *"If anyone teaches otherwise and does not consent to wholesome words, even the words of our Lord Jesus Christ, and to the doctrine which accords with godliness, he is proud, knowing nothing, but is obsessed with disputes and arguments over words, from which come envy, strife, reviling, evil suspicions, useless wrangling of men of corrupt minds and destitute of the truth, who suppose that godliness is a means of gain. From such withdraw yourself. "1 Timothy 6:3-5 (NKJV)*

Drunkenness – Intoxicated, *"Wine is a mocker, strong drink is raging and whoever is deceived by it is not wise."* Proverbs 20:1

Carousing – a night time frolicking of drunken behavior. Also known as a nighttime festival to the Greek god Bacchus.

This list and its definitions give insight into the thinking of the one, usually an adult child, that has found egregious fault with their family or a member of their family to the point of exiling the family.

God asked his family, the nation Israel, if anything like this had ever been seen before, they exchange a living supreme being for the hewn wood and rock of their own hands for their gods. (Jeremiah 10:3-8). For a family suffering through estrangement, the question is the same.

Why trade a loving supportive family for _____? (Fill in the blank because they traded their family for something.)

In some cases, it is for a lover, or a lifestyle, or like the prodigal son for freedom from morality. Whatever, the reason, the estranger left a family because of its warts to become a part of another life. Being in church does not nullify the deeds of the flesh committed against one's family. Even if they are still in church and teaching a Sunday School class they have left their spiritual foundation for the deeds of the flesh.

3
Reasons

For my people have committed two kinds of evil, they have forsaken the fountain of living waters, to hew for themselves cisterns, broken cisterns that cannot hold water. Jeremiah 2:13

GOD TELLS HIS people they are committing two evils. They are separating from God and seeking other gods. These two are the reasons the Israelites are estranging from their God, the one and only true God. In the same way, estranged family members have forsaken their family either one member or all of them in order to find something else or to join with something else.

The poetic imagery in the verse show the forsaking the fountain of living water, as the pure water of God's Word. Jesus Christ calls himself the living water in John 4:13 when Jesus tells the woman at the well, *"Everyone who drinks of this water will thirst again, but whoever drinks of the water that I will give him shall never thirst; but the water that I will give him will become in him a well of water springing up to eternal life."* This illustrates how the Israelites rejected God's method of reconciliation.

The term living water can refer to a live spring where fresh water bubbles up from the ground clean, cool and fresh. When Jesus spoke of a living water, it created this image.

A cistern is a manmade water collection system. It is a large tub near the slope of the roof of a house. Usually covered with a straining type of material to catch leaves, bugs, and dirt from the roof. Rain water falls into the cistern, giving the household a source of water for drinking as well as cleaning. Many times the tub will be built of wood that will expand causing water leakage. It can also be made of a concrete lined bowl in the ground to catch the water. Either way the cistern almost always leaks. A broken cistern allowed debris into the water.

In poetic form, God says, you have rejected the best I gave you for a system built with your own hands with many weak points causing the debris of the world to infiltrate the drinking water. Jesus is the pure water of the fountain, (John 7:37-39) and the world's idols built to the foreign gods with human hands are the cisterns.

Who and What Are These Gods?

Jeremiah 10 provides details of other gods. Before the other gods in Israel can be explored, one must ask the question, 'how did the gods get into Israel?' In the same way a family asks, what tore apart the family relationships, and how did it enter into the Christian family unit? Why haven't churches recognized and addressed the problem?

Roman 15:4 tells us the things that were written earlier were for our instruction and edification to give us a hope in Christ. Therefore, we turn to the history of Israel to discover the character of God in the case of the estranged family.

God raised a nation of His own from one man Abraham. From him came Isaac, the son whom He loved, from Isaac came Jacob the father of the twelve tribes and from Jacob came Joseph who spent his life in an Egyptian jail. Nonetheless, he became the salvation for the seventy descendants of Jacob, which made up the entire Hebrew nation at the time. As they moved into the land of Goshen, they multiplied and lived fruitfully, until a new Pharaoh arose that did not know the contributions of Joseph. (Exodus 1:2). The new Pharaoh felt fearful of the Hebrew population and made them into slaves. There they remained as slaves for four hundred years, just as God had told Abraham would happen. (Genesis 15:13.) Then God raised Moses and trained him the first forty years of his life with the best education available as a son of the daughter of Pharaoh. The second part of Moses life he cared for sheep in the desert. The last forty years of Moses life he spent bringing the Hebrew nation of millions to the promised land of Israel. He knew how to lead ignorant sheep, now those same practices were being used to lead an ignorant people through the desert. It took forty years of wondering before they were allowed to enter the land. Upon entering, they were required to fight the Canaanites who occupied the land. Once God established them as the nation, Israel, He served as their governmental authority figure through the judges. The nation spent more than 300 years in a cycle of disobedience, calling out to God, being released from torment of surrounding nations and then returning to their wicked ways of worshiping false gods.

    Samuel served as the last judge. As he incorporated his sons to take over the judgeship, the people rejected them. Samuel was upset at the turn of events, but his sons were worthless men and the people didn't want them for their leaders, they didn't trust them. They decided a king would be better. Samuel felt rejection by the people he loved and whom he led for forty years. Then God told Samuel the people were rejecting Him, not Samuel. (1 Samuel 8:9-22)

God knew the people no longer wanted to be a theocracy but wanted to have a human leader, even in spite of the warnings about the nature of human kings. (Deuteronomy 17:14-20) God selected Saul and Samuel anointed him as king (1 Samuel 10:1). God touched his heart and changed him into a leader, (1 Samuel 10:9).

That is until Saul's gross disobedience. Then he lost the kingship and his mind. (1 Samuel 15:10 -11). David was appointed by God and took the throne of Hebron for seven years before he became king over all Israel. David ruled forty years as a fair and just king.

David wanted to build a temple for the Ark of the Covenant, after he brought the Ark back to Israel from the Philistines. He found an architect to draw up the plans. He gathered the materials to build, nonetheless, his son Solomon served as overseer of the building of the temple. After four years as king, Solomon spent the next seven years of his forty-year reign building the temple which David wanted to build. David was unable to do so because of being a man of war and shed blood. (1 Chronicles 28:2-3).

Sadly, after the temple was dedicated Solomon became a political negotiating figure head to which many nations brought their daughters to him for wives and concubines. He ended up with 1000 women in his life from all the surrounding nations. He also built stables and had many horses, which were animals of war and God specifically told him there would be peace during his tenure as king. Solomon should not multiply wives because they would turn his heart away from God. (Deuteronomy 17:14-20, 1 Samuel 11:4).

Solomon disobeyed and multiplied both horses and wives. The act of allowing these gods into Israel defied God's repeated warning about them. Not only did Solomon allow the gods and their altars to be built in Israel, he often worshiped at these altars with his various wives, allowing his own sons and daughters to be sacrificed to the gods; Chemosh, Molech and Milcom. He worshipped the goddess Ashtoreth. (1 Kings11:7) Solomon's heart turned away from God and was not wholly devoted to God as his father David's. (1 Kings 11:6-8). In response to his disobedience the kingdom was severed and Israel was given to Jeroboam to build the Northern kingdom of Ephraim or Israel.

His servant and two tribes, Judah and Benjamin stayed with Solomon's son Rehoboam and formed the southern kingdom of Judah (1 Kings 11:11).

There it is! Did you see it? The foreign gods entered into Israel through the wives and concubines of Solomon. A king who had the power and authority to keep them out instead he allowed their altars to be built on God's land and even worshiped at them. Notice the sad statement in chapter eleven verse nine, *"the Lord was angry with Solomon because his heart was turned away from the Lord God of Israel."* Even Solomon the wisest, wealthiest man to live estranged from his Father in order to worship the other gods. So how does this relate to the estranged family?

Before answering that question let's look at the gods listed that Solomon allowed into his kingdom. He took the daughter of Pharaoh and daughters from the Moabite, Ammonite, Edomite, Sidonian and Hittite women. These were the nations which brought the foreign gods into the land.

Daughter of Pharaoh would bring the Egyptian gods. There are more than 122 gods of Egypt at the time. Some of the names which are most familiar in modern times include, Ra, Osiris, Horus, Nut (creator) Anubis, (death), Thoth, (moon), Bes (medicine), Isis, (mother) and many more.

Other gods mentioned in Samuel:

- Astereth, goddess of the Sidonians
- Milcom detestable idol of the Ammonites, required human infant sacrifice for worship.
- Chemosh detestable idol of Moab, required human infant sacrifice.
- Molech detestable idol of Ammon, Required human infant sacrifice.

These gods required human sacrifice as part of their worship. (an act declaring Satan's hatred of humankind.) They were fertility gods and the worship included gross sexual activity, abuse of young girls and boys and the death of infants. All forms of sexual impurity took place such as homosexuality, gender bending and pedophilia. These were the gods Solomon allowed into Israel. Even though God spoke to Solomon twice and blessed him with wealth and wisdom. Solomon was not ignorant of the Lord God of his nation Israel. His actions indicate he followed the women he loved and didn't see harm in allowing them to worship their gods.

Modern Gods

There is the spirit of these same gods living among Christians and in Christian nations with the spirits sometimes incorporated into church programs. The doctrines of demons invade the hearts of church leaders as wisdom, causing these ideas to be adopted as philosophy into the preaching and teaching, leading church members astray.

Ashtoreth is represented today by Wicca and witchcraft. Other names used for "mother earth" are the goddesses Inanna, Ishtar, Diana, Venus, and a host of other names. Their symbols and images are used in logos and brands throughout the economic world. Currently there are more witches in the United States than there are Presbyterians and it is a growing religion.[9] Milcom, Chemosh and Molech were gods of sexual deviation and child sacrifice. In modern culture these gods are called abortion, homosexuality, transgenderism, pedophilia and animal love, another name for bestiality.

Although it is difficult to have numbers regarding the growth of Wicca it can be measured by the large numbers of teenage girls who embrace the pagan religion purchasing novels about witchcraft and spirituality. These novels teach spiritual growth in the Wiccan religion by using fantasy and romance.[10] The morality of these materials give young girls a moral and religious framework to develop their attitudes towards their feminine bodies and sexuality. This leads them into embracing the feminist movement which leads to the morality of abortion. The feminist movement provides interpretation and cultural significance to these young readers about witchcraft. The *Harry Potter* series advances witchcraft as the hero in the stories but it is only the beginning of the steady diet of positive witchcraft materials being fed to young people, especially girls. The books present stories that appeal to their fairness sensibilities and uses the books to teach them how to reject their parents Christianity.[11] Witchcraft walks into the church service every Sunday morning in the mind of the fourteen year old child who read a fantasy book the night before. Or with the parents who watched a television show glamorizing the occult. Witchcraft creeps into the church body to "turn the gospel of Christ into lasciviousness." (Jude 4).

Like Solomon we have allowed foreign gods into our land. The church has set the table for a host of other gods that have entered behind them. A look at any large city reveals their presence and their growing presence of temples built to worship the idols of Hinduism, Buddhism, Islam, secular humanism, New Age and a host of other Eastern religions beside the pagan gods.

How does this relate to the broken heart of the abandoned parent of an adult child or an adult abandoned by parents?

How can a biblical counselor teach the Old Testament as applicable to the life of the fourteen-year-old in the pew who knows more about witchcraft than they do the Bible?

The Hidden Gods

Paul addresses the other gods in 1 Corinthians 10 when he says, "I don't want you to be unaware. . ." Then he proceeds to relate the history of the birth of the nation Israel as they left slavery in Egypt to travel across the wilderness to the promised land of Israel. Paul addresses four things. The "baptism into Moses in the cloud" which establishes Moses authority as their leader because he submits to the authority of the cloud which is God's leadership. The necessities of life are addressed in the phrase, spiritual food, which refers to the manna and quail God provided for them. The water given them in the midst of the desert came from the rock that Moses struck. This rock follows them throughout their journey and Paul references Christ as the spiritual water that gives life. The phrase "nevertheless" presents a strong word of contrast which says, the above mentioned is true, but this is also true, "God is not well-pleased." Even though they were all on this journey together as one congregation, God was not pleased with many of them and the next sentence should make one's hair stand at attention. "They were laid low in the wilderness." This congregation that is being addressed are the freed slaves. They will all die in the desert except for two, Joshua and Caleb. The second generation enters Israel. God's displeasure with our activities carry a grave consequence. This is a prime example of living one's Christian freedom without recognition of one's Christian responsibility.

This large group of people came out of a pagan society with a god to address every human question of origin and physics. Paul is reminding the people the escape from Egypt was not just a physical escape from slavery but also a spiritual escape from the vile cruelty of Egyptian gods and their worship. Yet, even with the miraculous rescue of a nation, they still brought the images of those gods with them. They still called upon those gods. They didn't trust the God of their nation even when He revealed His marvelous love for them through His power of rescue and provision.

God is not pleased with them even though they were all drinking of the same water from the rock Moses struck. Paul is teaching this same principle to the people in Corinth, a port city filled with pagan gods and temples. The Christians there are a minority and they are battling the politically correct society of idolatry and paganism, with God's message of love and responsibility by regarding His laws of morality. The gods of Corinth demanded gross sexual immorality and child sacrifice. The message of the one true God is foreign to the culture and to the sinful nature of every man.

Standing firm in the Word of God is not easy. It is almost impossible in a culture that condemns every belief and action of the Christian life by turning the truth into a lie and leading the nation to worship the carved images of creatures rather than the creator. (Romans 1). A glimpse at American society reveals an obsession with animals. So much so that pets are called children and people refer to themselves as the mother or daddy to a dog.[12] No human has ever given birth to a dog. Referring to an animal as one's child is the ultimate insult to the image of God. Yet, at the same moment one claims an animal as offspring, they condone the killing of human babies as a sacrifice to the god of pleasure and convenience. No wonder God is not pleased with them or us. No wonder our children are separating from family members when our society does not value their worth as God's most precious gift. How many times do parents refer to a family pet as the brother or sister of their children? Does the child then think the dog is an equal sibling? Only humans carry the breath of God and only humans are the children of humans. This seemingly innocent phraseology is a demonic mindset that devalues God's image in humankind.

Even in this culture the Christian must stand firm and the only way to do that is to have knowledge of one's history and belief system. To seek to know God by listening, watching and obeying His words. Paul refers to this when he says, "Now these things happened as examples for us, so that we would not crave evil things as they also craved." 1 Corinthians 10:6.

Crave evil things! Think on that for a minute. What does it mean? What are the evil things one craves and from where does the craving come? Paul explains this by reliving some of the idolatrous acts the people committed in the wilderness. He says "Do not be idolaters as some of them were."

What were they craving? The pleasure of the flesh. In the event of the golden calf they were desiring the sexual immorality and impurity they had experienced back in Egypt. The sexual orgies and sexual perversion was practiced for the pleasure of the gods. The scripture says,' they ate and rose to play.' That play was not a game of dominos.

Paul gives another reminder that the events occurred as an example and for our instruction. What is the instruction an estranged family can derive from Paul's examples?

It is the simple premise of staying in the Word of God and cleansing the spirit with the pure water of the word. (Ephesians 5:26). It will prevent one from falling into idolatry and following the destructive ways of the prince of the world. (I John 5:19).

Sexual Deviation

The estrangement may occur while seeking the pleasure of the flesh. It may be a relationship that is contrary to the family's standards or the desire to participate in a sexual lifestyle that is not pleasing to the family, or curiosity. The estranger wants to experience some of the world's offerings without guilt. By separating from a Christian family and taking a relationship to "no contact," the estranger can participate in a sinful lifestyle without guilt or further guilt placement. The same principle applies to loans, inheritance and other money situations.

In this case the one left must be prepared by Galatians 6, to bear one another's burdens and to correct gently. For the person escaping the guilt effects of a Christian family will return with much destruction. (1 Corinthians 5:5) The devil will eviscerate the individual before allowing them to return to a loving family where they will see the grace of Christ displayed. However, this same damage will also drive the sexually wayward family member back to the family and toward the forgiving grace of Christ.

Grumbling

The biblical picture of grumbling which Paul addresses can be found in Numbers 21:5, *"The people spoke against God and "Why have you brought us up out of Egypt to die in the wilderness? For there is no food and no water, and we loathe this miserable food." Numbers 21:5*

This food was given as a picture of Christ as the living bread, (John 6:31-35). When the people stated their distaste for the food, God removed his protection from the natural dangers of the wilderness and allowed the poisonous snakes to rise and bite the people. The verse ends with a strange statement, *"destroyed by the destroyer."* In order to identify the destroyer, one can review the rebellion of Korah found in Numbers 16.

This event illustrates the jealousy of siblings. When the Levites Korah, Dathan and Abiram challenged Moses' authority, God said to them, *"You have gone far enough for all the congregation is holy, every one of them, and the Lord is in their midst, so why do you exalt yourself above the assembly of the Lord." Numbers 16:3.* The lecture continues in verse 9, *"Is it not enough for you that the God of Israel has separated you from the rest of the congregation of Israel, to bring you near to Himself, to do the service of the tabernacle of the LORD, and to stand before the congregation to minister to them?"*

The siblings grumbling against one another miss the message; grumbling is against the parents, not the siblings. This grumbling will contribute or cause a family estrangement. While the vocal dissatisfaction is against a sibling, it will be used to discredit the parent for treating them differently. Yet, God tells them, I set you apart for a special service for which you were designed. In the same way, parents see the different personalities and talents of their children. It is not expected to have cookie-cutter children each doing the same or even looking the same. The overweight child is just as precious to a parent as the trim athletic child. This reveals the danger of adult children blaming mom and dad of partiality.

Moses makes it clear their grumbling against Aaron as high priest is a charge against the Lord. In this instance God's displeasure against Korah, Dathan, and Abiram results in the earth opening up and swallowing them alive. God gives parents the authority to raise their children in the knowledge of Him, (Ephesians 6:4, Hebrews 12:7-8) The child who abandons the parent over partiality is in disobedience to God, in the same way as Korah, Dathan and Abiram. They are also in the same danger, they may cut off a parent and destroy a life God intended for them to have; a life with grandparents to help love and raise children in a world growing darker daily, a life with an unmovable support source no matter whether the child is right or wrong.

The adult child who abandons themselves from their loving Christian parents will see problems such as health, finances, rebellious children open in their lives to swallow them alive into Sheol. (depression, financial strife, legal problems etc.) An adult child separating from their parents should be warned of the danger of their actions. Unfortunately, many do not weigh the consequences of their actions and since the reconciliation statistics reveal a small number, there are few who share their experiences of loss and problems as a result of their action.[13] This is how the grumbler is destroyed by the destroyer. The sin of grumbling will itself destroy the person.

Timing

An analogy or an application of scripture cannot always be applied in the literal sense but may be applied in the spiritual sense. The lesson from this history lesson Paul is teaching, shows the timing of attack occurs at a moment of weakness when it is least expected. Estrangement occurs as a surprise to the Christian. It causes great delight among the demonic world to leave a bleeding wound on one of God's children, allowing that wound to infect future generations.

Whatever event occurs causing estrangement, there will be a timing issue. I feel my daughter was about to embark upon a writing career leading people into a study of God's word. What better way to prevent ministry than to question one's history with a family member? This questioning in the mind turns the spirit of a loving family into an abusive family, due to mistakes made by family members. (Romans 3:23). The blunders made in the past provide material for the serpent and his minions to use against the tired, spiritually struggling member and make them turn against their firmest support and unconditional love of their family. Only a family structure is able to provide unconditional love that will mirror the everlasting lovingkindness of the Father. In fact, this is the primary role of a family. What better way to stop a ministry than to put bitterness into the heart of the minister in regard to their family? This very act distorts the plan of God for His children.

A healthy life can be built with the energy used to justify and explain one's actions within or without the family. Estrangement causes damage to the people involved. The circumstances nor the event which caused the estrangement matter. The loss of will to live and thrive comes as a result of the deep anguishing pain without any release or a talent is wasted while one nurtures their anger and victimhood. People suffering estrangement know they must build new lives without the other. It's the only way to survive the pain. Both parties must become healthy before reconciliation can occur.[14]

History

But wait a minute! 1 Corinthians 10:13 says God will not give us more than we can bear. Right? That's a portion of the promise but not the promise. The word used is temptation. It relates to destruction. There are three sources of temptation addressed in the New Testament these are;

- Human sin nature
- Personal evil (the demonic)
- The fallen world system (Ephesians 2:1-3, James 4:1,4,7)

The first sentence says, what you are going through is experienced by all people in one of the three ways listed above. Even an estrangement can be manifested by one of those three sources.

This declaration is followed by a profound truth, "God is faithful!" If nothing else in this text relates to you the reader, remember this statement. It will carry you through the trial you are facing. This is the promise made. It's not about what we can bear or endure, it is about the faithfulness of God while we are enduring the trial.

The next sentence offers hope, "a way of escape." The Greek meaning of this word refers to a military unit and implies one does not travel through this trial alone. Does this mean some will escape the pain of estrangement and others won't? Yeah! Even though this is hard to swallow, there is no promise the estranged family will ever reconcile during the earthly journey of life.[15] Don't give up hope, because even though we cannot know the ways of God, we know without any doubt,

He will not leave us. No matter what the family member does. (Psalm 23:4). In that promise we live.

In the context of God's word, this escape for one who is estranged will be the family unit. It will be difficult for the family unit to come together in forgiveness and restoration and the relationship will most likely never be what it once was. However, the new relationship may be more beneficial to the kingdom of God. Therefore, be ready to accept one who has left the family unit, or to be accepted by the family unit one left.

4
Demons

JEREMIAH REFERS TO the idols as the objects of His children's affection. (Jeremiah 5:7) A comparison of adultery to idolatry indicate the depth of depravity one falls when worshiping the wooden idol representing a god. Paul uses the term 'demons' to refer to the same gods.

The gods are spiritual beings that do not live in the physical realm of humanity but they do have some ability to interfere with mankind.[16] 1 John 5:19 tells us "the whole world lies in the power of the devil." The Bible provides information we need to know to overcome the influence of demons.

Because the gods were ingrained so deep in Corinth Paul found it necessary to teach the young Christians about the influence of demons. This information is viable for the young and the mature Christian wondering about demonic influence in life.[17] It cannot be taken lightly but at the same time it is not the focus either of Paul's teaching or of this teaching. It is a reality that must be addressed in the knowledge of Scripture. Let me first admonish you the reader that this is not a method of "rebuking" the demons. It is the belief of this author that only Jesus Christ is capable of rebuking the spiritual beings. Peter warns us about railing against the angels and Luke gives the details of frivolous encounter with a cleaver and strong spiritual being in Acts 19.

A priest rebuked the demons in Ephesus and finds himself naked and beaten.

Demons are incredibly evil and equally deceptive. Like their father, the devil, they are liars and when they speak it is always a lie (Jn 8:44.) This is why God admonishes His people to be knowledgeable of the Word of God for it is the only weapon we are given to fight demons. (Ephesians 6:10).

Paul begins his treatise in regard to demons when he says, "Therefore, my brethren flee from idolatry." In other words, do not indulge in those things which give honor and recognition to the demons. By fleeing from the images and practices of idol worship of the demons, one will not be deceived.

Paul gives this same warning to his listeners which he calls wise men, (2 Corinthians 11:19) probably with a sarcastic tone in his voice. He tells them to be discerning and judge what Paul says. In other words, Paul is telling them to measure his words against the words of the Old Testament, which is the Bible of this church.

As Paul builds his argument to strengthen the command to flee from idolatry, he starts with Christ by addressing the act of communion. He calls it the cup of blessing which means to praise or benefit, it is the Greek term, *Eulogia* and the basis for the term eulogy.[18] The blessing is a reminder we share in the sacrifice of Christ, allowing us to be reconciled to the Father. Why would he start here? Because Paul is about to address an issue of eating meat sacrificed to the demon idols and explain the communion with demons.

He draws attention to the nation Israel. Why? There are questions about the food sacrifice made to the images of the other gods. Many worshipers of the one and only God of Israel eat of the meat sacrificed to an idol. Paul is rebuking some of the frivolous ideas of holiness while at the same time revealing the problem of synergism.[19]

God gave Israel the blessing of the law which is the physical manifestation of Christ, (Matthew 5:17) fulfilling the law. Christ became the sacrifice once for all. (Hebrews 9:11-12). Jesus is both the fulfillment of the law and the sacrifice of atonement for sinners. Communion is an illustration of Christ's work on the cross given as a blessing in the gift of life in God's eternal family. Our eternal life came with a high price because of our estrangement from God due to the human sinful nature.

Paul takes this illustration of Christ's sacrifice first for the nation Israel and then for Christ-followers. At this time most Christians were Jews so they understood the illustration of the nation Israel and the sacrifices made yearly for atonement of sins. They could understand the sacrifice of Jesus on the cross once for all as the culmination of those ritual sacrifices that had been made since the days of the tabernacle and the wandering in the desert. This was not a mystery to them. (Romans 1:3-4).

On the other hand, Jews were ignorant of the ways of the other gods. The evil liars used their ignorance to confuse them. The arguments kept the Christians busy arguing between themselves, creating a lack of belief in Christ. Paul teaches that partaking of the communion meal is a symbol of sharing in the sacrifice of Jesus. It is the imparting of the sacrifice to the sinner through the body and blood of Christ. Therefore, if the communion is sharing in Christ's suffering what is it when one shares the meal offered to one of the other gods.

Humm! Paul is just beginning to address the problem of demonic influence on the Christian and the Jew. The context helps find the meaning in Paul's message.

Sacrifice to Demons

Let's take a left turn back to 1 Corinthians 8:1. Paul opens his discussion by saying, "Now, concerning the things sacrificed to idols." He is about to give teaching and instruction on how demonic influence comes into our lives and what we must do to protect ourselves from it.

The second sentence of verse one is meaningful to the members of an estranged family, *"we know that we have knowledge. Knowledge makes one arrogant but love edifies."*

Wow! Knowledge makes a person arrogant. The estranged family understands that statement. What kind of knowledge? It appears Paul is speaking about knowledge of the idols or gods (1 Corinthians 8:4).

Paul states it plainly, those who know God, the one and only God know true love and are known by Him; a relationship. One that God desires to have with His children. God wants a family. What do idols want? Idols are nothing but the works of man's hands. How can they want anything or give anything? Paul even says the sacrifice to idols is worthless, it means nothing, for there is not another God. Nonetheless, he warns there are many gods. Is this a contradiction?

No, it is a warning that even though there is only one true God there are many spiritual beings who are imitators. These imitators desire adoration and worship. Worship to other gods is given in the form of food and sex. A worthless idol cannot eat food, but the food is symbolic in the worship. Once the worship is finished the food can be sold at a public market. Paul is addressing that food that has been sacrificed to these idols. Since they are wooden is there anything wrong with the food?

The knowledge to which Paul refers in verse 1 Corinthians 8:1 could be discernment based on the knowledge of the One True God. It makes no difference to God whether His children eat the food or not. It was created and given by God to man. This is the knowledge of the food, all good things come from God. God knows people have need of nourishment. There is no spiritual power attached to the food. It is still the basic elements of nourishment, proteins, carbohydrates, fats, minerals and vitamins. It will nourish the body. The one who has knowledge of God knows this. The weaker person who puts his trust in the block of wood believes the spiritual imbues something mystical into the meat, therefore, if a Christian eats of the meat then the weak one will assume they are worshipping the god to whom it was offered.

By eating the meat, a Christian may prevent the non-Christian from obtaining the knowledge of Jesus that can save them. This idea of eating meat sacrificed to an idol is continued in chapter 10 of First Corinthians. There is an important point made in verses 19-20, *"Do I mean that a thing sacrificed to idols is anything or that an idol is anything?"*

Paul is declaring that the meat sacrificed to a worthless idol is nothing but there is a spirit behind that idol and that spirit is a demon. Therefore, the picture relates the connecting of idols with demons. If a Christian sacrifices anything to a demon, they cannot sit at the table with Jesus.

Paul has associated the sacrifice of Jesus to the communion meal. So now, does this same principle apply to idols? Of course not, the idol is nothing more than a block of wood with a few rhinestones on it. Paul warns in verse twenty that the spirit behind that idol is a demon and when an idol is given the same reverence of heart as the communion then one is sharing a meal with demons.

If a Christian is worried about the meat being endowed with spiritual power, then he is giving worship to the demon to whom it was sacrificed. The worship comes from the heart, not from the idol. In other words, the meat has no effect upon the one with knowledge of Jesus, unless they consider the demons equal to Jesus. In that case they will be unable to sit at the communion table of Christ.

One cannot sit at the table and offer reverence to a demon and take communion too. Yet, many try. This occurs in the church even today. This is synergism. The practice of taking beliefs from other religions and incorporating it into a Christian theme. The problem Paul is addressing is the meat market. A routine every day event to go to the meat market and buy food for the family meal. Yet, there is controversy due to lack of understanding. Paul is walking a delicate line attempting to teach new Jewish Christians the value of the law and the truth of grace. The Gentiles are those holding pagan beliefs in other gods. They sacrifice their best stock and offer the meat to the idol. Then the priests of the demon gods gather the prime meat and sell it at a market. What a scheme! Convince the people they will receive peace if they give their best and most expensive stock to this wooden block of wood. Once the worshipper is gone, the priest takes the meat and sells it to the Christian. There is no overhead expense only profit. The controversy may have arisen because of the unfair market prices, but whatever the cause, the Jews felt concern since the heart of the Gentile offered it as a gift to the demon spirit behind the idol.

This same thing is taking place in churches all across America. One such practice is called "Christian Yoga." Other infiltrations of idolatry in the church include; Christian Tarot Cards, Christian Angel boards (same as Ouija boards). It is being offered in healing processes known as Chakras, Reiki, Incense, etc. [20] Even more than the infiltration of paganism into church programs is the invasion of a practice known as mindfulness or meditation into schools and businesses. While a family may believe they are fully sold out to Christ they may be letting the spirit of a demon come into the home through objects used by the demon spirit under the guise of being Christian or educational.[21]

The demon influence will not use that which is obvious, but that which can be construed as good. For instance, parents felt it was good their kids were reading *Harry Potter*, at least they were reading.[22] Yet the books focused on witchcraft as the hero and allowed the spirit of witchcraft to enter into the child's thinking. This would leave a child with an open door to a demon to enter into the child's will and emotions. Many Christian mothers helped their children dress up as

Harry Potter and go see the movies.[23] For younger children the Pokémon game taught young children to fight each other to the death and then go to the spiritual hospital and be reincarnated.

Self-Esteem and Estrangement

Self-esteem is the demon spirit behind the idol of "loving myself, so I can love others." Church programs, school teachers and parents felt this new type of parenting and teaching would raise well balanced children and produce confident adults. Instead, the movement of "thinking highly of oneself." (Romans 12:3) called self-esteem takes Christ out of the equation causing one to focus on their emotions rather than sound judgment. Jay Adams wrote a text about the phenomenon in 1986.

> "To get an accurate picture of how widespread and far-reaching the self-esteem movement is. It is not simply a passing fad. It has been coming on slowly for a long time, but now that it is here, it has suddenly assumed proportions far greater than anyone could have predicted and has attained so large a place in the thinking of many Christian leaders. . . we can be sure its teaching will have impact on the church not only in this generation but in the next as well. . .. this phenomenon is not something isolated within the church but is broadly accepted and propagated in non-Christian circles as well. . .. liberals, nonbelievers, and Bible-believing Christians alike are caught up in the self-esteem movement."[24]

The parents led their children to the table of demons expecting to find Christ in their self-esteem. Sunday School and youth departments programs entertained them. Teachers and youth ministers were recruited based on their ability to connect with the youth. Children's teachers were given a simplistic teachers guide to follow filled with games and cute stories. In all the efforts to reach the generation raised on good self-esteem, the Scripture was often ignored or given a cursory acknowledgement with a memory verse at the beginning of the class. The scripture warned about the devastating effects of elevating oneself to the level of a god.

> *"Then you will remember your evil ways and your deeds that were not good, and you will loathe yourselves in your own sight for your iniquities and your abominations. Ezekiel 36:31*
>
> *"If I speak with the tongues of men and angels, and have not love I am as a noisy gong or clanging cymbal." 1 Corinthians 13:1*
>
> *"Behold, I was brought forth in iniquity, and in sin my mother conceived me." Psalm 51:5*
>
> *"Your ways and your deeds have brought these things to you. This is your evil. How bitter! How it has touched your heart!" Jeremiah 4:18,*

J.I. Packer wrote, "… Christians spread a thin layer of Bible teaching over the mixture of popular psychology and common sense. … their overall approach reflects the narcissism or the selfish or meism."[25]

Now this demon can demand worship from those children trained in self-esteem in the form of estranging from parents because they do not have the knowledge of the true God and they have become arrogant in their self-esteem and their self-knowledge which is used to regulate their emotions. The common phrase used by adult children about their justification for estranging from their parents is spoken without evidence of wrong-doing but rather a nebulous accusation such as, "they ruined my life." With the self-esteem movement of the 80's another foundational layer is added to develop a more destructive tool in deconstructing God's plan.

To illustrate, look at the chart to see family development in the recent past decades;

Process of Family Deconstruction	
1950	Growth of Prosperity
1960	Free-Love, Abundant material goods, growth of drug-abuse, second-wave feminism
1970	Divorce, Govn't support for single parents, Legal Abortion; disposable human babies
1980	Blended families, Grandparents as parents, Self-esteem movement
1990	Domestic violence, increased child abuse, homosexual movement
2000	Equality in the sexes, fluid gender, Disposable or multiple fathers
2010	Estrangement, disposable grandparents
2020	?

A church, a family, a school, a society or a culture cannot sit at the table with demons and expect to participate in the communion meal with Christ to receive His salvation from the schemes of the devil. These schemes are a cause of the Christian argument regarding communion with Christ to lose credibility, even among strong Christians. Due to the heavy influence of these things such as yoga and Harry Potter in American society, it is difficult to think of them as demonic influence.[26]

Paul dealt with these same attitudes as he attempts to help the people understand why God was not well-pleased with the Israelites coming out of Egypt. God was not well-pleased with the synergism or the self-deification or self-esteem. God is still not well-pleased with the synergism in modern church congregations.

Paul attempts to teach the new Christians that the problem is not the eating of the meat rather the sharing in the worship of demons by participating in demonic influential activities that causes one to have communion with the devil. It is wise to note that the demonic influence can enter the mind through media and set dormant for years.

When the proper trigger is applied, demonic activity will enter the mind as truth. All these ideas were implanted in the heads and hearts of Christian families in such a manner they were often unaware of the invasion. Therefore, when Christian young people raised at the table of demons grew older they were primed and ready for the assault of a demonic spirit to control their thinking.

Paul said he could eat the meat sacrificed to an idol with no problem, BUT, if it caused someone to stumble to see him eat it, then he would not eat it. In the same way, Christians who are not susceptible to a hidden demonic influence should not participate in activities that could cause a brother or sister to stumble in their developing faith. Paul's final admonishment on this topic is:

    1. Partake of the meat with thankfulness to God,

    2. If one serves it and makes note that was offered to an idol or
a   god, do not eat it.

    3. Whatever you eat or drink, give glory to God

    4. Do not offend anyone with the issue.

Number four tells us not to condemn people for their participation in activities with demonic influence. This does not mean we do not warn others about the danger and provide the warning with a hope that will lead them to salvation. For example; if a friend is participating in a Yoga class and beginning to experience some mental problems, they could be experiencing demonic influence. Perhaps suggesting a program of stretches designed by a physical therapist rather than a yoga practitioner may help their mental state. The ministry is to lead them to salvation, not condemnation. (Romans 8:1-2)

Paul is warning the new Christians about the subtleness of the demons. Their greatest trick is to be invisible and to convince Christians they are not present or don't exist at all. This was Paul's warning. Those who have knowledge become arrogant in their own knowledge, not in the ways of God. Those who attempt to control thoughts while participating in the knowledge of demons in an entertaining form find themselves in the midst of migraines, nightmares, depression, etc. The demon influence has infiltrated the mind and only the work of Christ can disperse the demons. Once the Word of God enters the mind and heart of a Christian, the demonic influence will be recognized by the one suffering and they find the escape from evil. "Therefore, flee from idolatry." (1 Corinthians 10:14) In short, Paul teaches them to stop doing that activity that allows the demonic influence in one's mind. It is the only way to protect oneself and family from demonic influence.

Warning

Paul is relating to a Christian church in First Corinthians. He warns about the everyday events of life that become tools for demonic influence. Because once they are allowed to enter the spirit they change the thinking and the condition of the heart.

Once a deception takes root it will draw an innocent person into an activity that harbors demonic influence. The activity is seen as an invitation into that life, it will take hold and will not let go. However, it will hide in such a manner that often a family continues with their church attendance, Sunday school teachings, Bible Study class, fellowship and participating in mission activities and all the while carrying a demonic influence in their spirit, unawares. Maybe this is why Paul used the phrase, "I don't want you to be unaware."

Or, the influence may enter into a life through the influence of another person. The Christian that is tired and has been lax in their daily ingestion of the Word and neglectful of their prayer life will find themselves to be prime targets of demonic influence.

The demonic influence does not care about the non-Christian, he already has them fooled and they belong to Satan. It is the Christian with the godliest influence that will be the primary recruit for demonic infestation. This life is warfare for a Christian.

Often our comfort level in the safety of our church attendance and church friends' serves as a substitute for our weapons in the sword of the spirit and prayer. Hebrew 4:12 calls the word of God a two-edged sword able to separate bone from marrow. This is a formidable weapon; why would we possess so strong a weapon if we had a weak enemy?

The enemy seeks to devour. He is a murderer and a destroyer and his weapon is deception and his method of deconstructing God's plan is destruction of God's gift. What better way to attack his most prominent enemy than through that which is valued most by God and thus by His children – the family!

5
God's Plan

MOST EVERY CHRISTIAN has said at some time or another, "God has a plan." What does that mean? Do we know His plan? Can we know His plan? Then we ask, "If He has a plan why is my family fractured?"

All of these are viable questions which every Christian should ask at one time or another is the state of their walk with Christ. It is important to note that all Christian beliefs must be grounded in the Word of God, which is about His love, because *God is love*, (1 John 4:4.)

Without solid ground upon which to give our answers Christians can be confused causing one to turn against God when the simple learned answers fail due to lack of understanding or misinterpretation.[27] Therefore, the next chapter is going to look at the message of the Bible. You may read some strange things, but I advise you to take the time to look up the scriptures listed in the explanation and to pray over them, take the counsel of the Holy Spirit. He is your teacher and when He speaks He speaks truth, (1 John 3:27, Psalm 1:1-2).

The Beginning

In the beginning, God! (Genesis 1:1 and John 1:1) In that statement we see the plan of God laid out in the form of the written word. Understanding comes with the exposure of God's plan in the remainder of His book.

Then why is it so hard to understand? This is a viable question. God didn't make the message of His word confusing, He made it an adventure with Him. This is why the study of the Word is peaceful and directive. It is spending time with our Father teaching us. He knew we could not absorb the whole plan as spiritual infants so He laid it out in such a way that we absorb more knowledge as we grow. (Isaiah 28:13). Just as physical growth adds to knowledge every year of a person's life, so it is with spiritual growth.

In the same manner a loving parent holds their child in their lap and reads a story book to them, so God holds us in His lap and reads the simple story to us. He is loving us as He reveals the story. God faces a problem with teaching us when we won't crawl in His lap, quiet our play time and listen to the story and His explanation.

In the first two chapters of the book of Genesis, God reveals the story of our creation and our home. Did you ever know a child that didn't love to hear about his birth and homecoming? How the family gathered around and watched him stretch and yawn and each made comments about how much the new baby looked like another family member. So it is with God, each time a new infant is born into His kingdom the angels gather and admire the new family member. (1 Peter 1:12)

The angels peer into the things of the physical realm of mankind and marvel at their human cousins. They are like them in that they share the same father, but different since humans are the image of the Father. In the simplest form, God wants to have a family with the spiritual beings and His human creation. He wants to talk to them, to teach them, to spend time with them. He wants to create good things for them. He wants to love them and be loved by them. God wants a family!

There it is. **God's plan** ![28] To build a family that loves Him. The rest of the Bible relates incidents of trials in this pursuit of a family and how God the Father handles them. It is always in love, even His wrath is the depth of an eternal unconditional love revealed. "God is love." (1 John 4:8). The one who does not love, does not know God.

How do we know this is His plan? When God creates man, He blows His breath into the nostril of the lump of clay which He forms with his own hands. Everything else was spoken into existence, but man was formed. His life is the essence of God. Only man has the breath of God, therefore, only man is the child of God, made in His image, created for His good pleasure. The first commandment God gives to His creation is multiply and care for the earth; the home which He created for His family.

Even the wickedness of man does not change God's plan as He gives Noah the same command after the flood. The plan was interrupted by the pride and deception of Satan. How do we know the serpent in Genesis 3 is Satan? Because Revelation 12:7 identifies him as the serpent of old. It appears the supernatural beings known as angels were living side by side with man in the garden and could interact with them.

If this is true, then why would the serpent tempt the woman? The answer to that question lies in Genesis 1:28 and Isaiah 14: 13-14. "God blessed them (Humans) and told them to subdue and rule over the earth and everything in it." God gave the earth to His human children. The serpent or Satan wanted to rule. In Isaiah 14:13, reveals his desire, *"I will ascend to heaven; I will raise my throne above the stars of God and I will sit on the mount of assembly in the recesses of the north, I will ascend above the heights of the clouds; I will make myself like the Most High."* Satan wants power and adoration.

That's right, Satan wants to be adored and be as powerful as God. What better way to achieve this goal than to take the rightful power of the earth from the children of God. The rightful heirs of creation.

However, children who trust a parent cannot be easily dissuaded to give away their hereditary rights. Therefore, Satan had to be "clever." He set up his plan of deception in the garden.

First he discredited God's provision, "Did God make all these trees and then tell you not to eat of them?" She responded with God's words, "No, only don't eat of the tree in the middle or we would die."

Now the serpent has her attention. He gives his second and third lie. "you will not surely die." The serpent is casting doubt on the integrity of God. Then the sneaky snake lays low and says, "He knows that if you eat of that tree you will become like gods." Bam! His plan is complete. Temptation enters. The smooth words of a lie make the fruit of that particular tree desirable. The serpent softly and cunningly pushes her to take the fruit of the forbidden tree and when she does she shares with Adam. At that moment, Satan steals the keys of power over the earth from mankind. In 1 John 5:19, the truth of the scene is stated, *"We know that the whole earth lies in the power of the evil one."*

This is not the end of God's plan. He had a back-up. When the man and woman hid themselves from God, it is evident they know they can no longer stand in His presence. He is holy and perfect and they are disobedient children.

What would an earthly parent do in such a case? Most likely in a loving home, the parent would scold and punish the rebellious act by showing the child the damage that has been done then pronounce punishment for the deed not a curse upon the child. God the Father illustrated a fundamental parenting technique? He searched for them, knowing where they were and what they had done, but making them face their disobedience. Then He provided clothing for them from the skin of animals. (Genesis 3:21). For the first time they see death and feel the sting of their disobedience. God is a loving parent to His children. Instead of punishment He covers them and tells them the consequences of their disobedience. He doesn't mention the loss of the rule over the earth, instead, he tells the man he will toil over the earth to provide sustenance for himself and his family. Now, man must conquer the wild earth rather than rule over it. The woman will be the mother of all things and nurture growth through the pain of childbirth and child rearing. The serpent is cursed along with the ground which he stole from the children. Then the final blow comes when the man and woman are told to leave this place known as home. Because of their deeds, perfection no longer exist. They now live in a world hostile to them because that world is now ruled by the serpent, who hates them. The evil one gains the power it craved, but not the adoration.

Worship of The Serpent

The deceiver with power over the air (Ephesians 2:2) saw an opening to plant his first seed of discontent in the heart of Cain, Adam and Eve's offspring. The act of jealousy is worship of the serpent. Cain became the weapon of the serpent against the Lord. The serpent is cursed and not happy with his lot. He can't change it. Nonetheless, it possesses the power to hurt God's children.

1 John 3:12 gives the reason. *Not as Cain, who was of the evil one and slew his brother. And for what reason did he slay him? Because his deeds were evil and his brothers were righteous.*

Making a sacrifice to God served the family as a means of worship to God. It provided a way of repentance for them. Hebrews 11:4 says that Abels was a better sacrifice because it was offered in faith. It doesn't say that Cain's sacrifice was unacceptable. The thing that was unacceptable to God was the condition of Cain's attitude, his desires, his heart.

The old lie of being like a god was used on Cain. God even asked Cain, "Why are you angry?" The no-regard for Cain's sacrifice was not an attack on Cain, it was a lesson for Cain to learn. Listen to God's voice as He speaks to Cain in Gen 4:6-7, *"Why are you angry? And why has your countenance fallen? "*

God is asking Cain, "What's wrong, what did I do to offend you?" Cain is angry at God. But God is gracious and loving when He speaks to Cain, "If you do well, will not your countenance be lifted up? And if you do not do well, sin is crouching at the door; and its desire is for you, but you must master it." Satan has turned Cain's heart away from loving God to adoring the deceiver in the act of worship through the murder of his brother. John 8:44 says, the devil is a liar and a murderer. God warned Cain.

Genesis 4:16 serves as one of the saddest scripture, *"And Cain went out from the presence of the Lord Gen 4:16.*

Cain reached a place of "no contact" with his family. Any person exiling their family and claiming 'no contact' is committing an act of worship of the devil. How can we draw this conclusion? Let's examine the words of the Lord closer.

The first question God asked Cain; Why are you angry? Every person who has experienced the loss of a family member due to estrangement has asked this same question. Most often there is no incident to cause the violent reaction. Instead there is violent sudden reaction of anger usually without any visible provocation.

Cain's reaction came by the fact God had no regard for Cain's sacrifice. What does no regard mean? The term 'regard' in Hebrew means to look at in dismay or disapproval. The scripture doesn't say why God was not pleased with the sacrifice except in Hebrews 11:4, "By faith Abel offered unto God a more excellent sacrifice than Cain. . ." It appears the condition of Cain's heart caused the "non-acceptance of his sacrifice. Cain didn't have faith in God, but rather in himself as preparing a proper sacrifice.

However, it doesn't say God didn't accept Cain. When Eve gave birth to Cain, she exclaimed, "I have a man-child with the help of the Lord." There is the possibility Eve thought Cain would be the Savior promised her in Genesis 3:15. The one who would restore the family to a right relationship with God. If this is the case, Cain grew up with prideful expectations. The failure of his sacrifice indicated his pride in his own value is misplaced. In this case Cain possessed a high self-esteem and could not listen to God's warning. Pride deceives and blinds. (Psalm 10:4, 73:6 Proverbs 11:2, 16:18, 29:23) God didn't love Cain less than Abel. God knew Cain needed to be cleansed of the same pride that caused the serpent to deceive the family in the first place. The final outcome of Cain's life is not known.

Cain chose to separate himself from God. He was not sent away, in fact God even put a protective plan around him by saying if anyone killed Cain they would face the vengeance of the Lord seven times.

If anyone dares to harm my daughter, I would be the big bad mama bear for her. I don't care if she never speaks to me or if I never see her again, I will not let anyone degrade her or harm her. I will suffer in silence rather than speak ill of my child.

If a human parent does this, how much more does a perfect Father with all power protect His children. God never rejected Cain, instead Cain rejected God. It appears there would have been forgiveness for the act of murder, if only he had admitted what he did and asked forgiveness. In the same way, estranged parents long for the adult child to return to the family.

Restoring The Family

Jeremiah 3:12 gives the steps of repentance. These steps are the same that must occur for a full restoration of an earthly family. These steps are the sole responsibility of the one who estranged themselves from the family unit. They must;

- Must admit their action of separating (Jeremiah 3:13)
- Repent of their separation (Jeremiah 3:14)
- Learn from counselors and wise teachers the value of preserving family. (Jeremiah 3:15)

Then they will be able to return to the family unit. As long as an estranged family member hold bitterness in his heart against the family they left, no restoration can take place. The one leaving is the only one that can restore the family. After they admit and recognize their departure from the family unit will reconciliation take place.

God says, "I will not be angry with you." By admitting one's estranging from the family, the departed one will be able to return to a family. Most likely there will be a great banquet of joy by the family and a welcoming home. The moment of a fallen countenance will be totally forgotten. A fallen countenance is difficult to overcome for the one departing but impossible for the hurting family to do it for them.

What is the countenance? It means the look on his face.[29] Any family that has been estranged by a family member knows exactly what the fallen countenance looks like. They saw it on the face of their loved one the moment the devil told them their family was their enemy. I remember seeing the look on my daughter's face and thinking, "Oh my gosh, I'm never going to see her again." It was obvious, her anger quickly built up into a vile hatred of me. It paralyzed me with fear.

The following statement has the power to freeze the blood with terror, "sin is crouching at your door; and its desire is for you."

When one becomes involved in worship of a demon, either in ignorance or with full knowledge, the demonic world will claim that person as their own.

A demon cannot enter a life except by invitation and anger is an invitation; especially anger with building hate capable of murder. Murder is the ultimate sacrifice of adoration of Satan. This is why God told Cain, 'You MUST master it." Jude 10-11 indicates Cain's reasoning was like a brute animal, what he knew naturally or instinctively, he corrupted himself. He didn't master the evil.

God's act of loving kindness toward Cain was the plea to reject the demon and return to God. When he didn't, his act of rebellion and rejection of his family is used throughout scripture as an example of rejection and evil.

> *Matthew 23:34-35," Therefore, I am sending you prophets and wise men and scribes; some of them you will kill and crucify, and some of them you will scourge in your synagogues and persecute from city to city so that upon you may fall the guilt of all the righteous blood shed on earth, from the blood of righteous Abel to the blood of Zechariah."*

The first murder is not forgotten with time but immortalized as the example of the shedding of innocent blood. Luke repeats this in

Luke 11:51," *"from the blood of Abel to the blood of Zechariah, it shall be charged against this generation."*

1 John 3:11-15 is the most condemning of all,

> *"For this is the message which you have heard from the beginning, that we should love one another; not as Cain, who was of the evil one and slew his brother. And for what reason did he slay him? Because his deeds were evil, and his brothers were righteous. Do not be surprised, brethren if the world hates you. We know that we have passed out of death into life, because we love the brethren. He who does not love abides in death." 1 Jn 3:11-15*

The one who estranges from his family follows the footsteps of Cain by giving adoration to the father of lies and murder, the devil. It is the measurement of one's devotion to God by how much one loves another. By estranging from a family, that one will be in the clutches of the demon either for eternity or until he masters the sin crouching at his heart's door.

This is harsh, no doubt. The idea that anyone who abandons family whether it be sibling, child or parent is the guilty party. This idea does not settle well, for there should be circumstances of abuse or sexual misconduct that gives the estranger the right to abandon the family. Scripture provides no allowance for an adult child to abandon a parent no matter what the circumstances. The commandment given is, "Honor your Father and Mother." It doesn't mean one has to love their parent, but honor is necessary. This commandment is followed by explanation in Exodus saying that anyone who curses father or mother should be put to death. (Exodus 21:15 & 17) What does this mean?

Paul addresses this concept to Timothy,

> "*All who are under the yoke as slaves are to regard their own masters as worthy of all honor so that the name of God and our doctrine will not be spoken against. Those who have believers as their masters must not be disrespectful to them because they are brethren, but must serve them all the more, because those who partake of the benefit are believers and beloved. Teach and preach these principles.*" (1 Timothy 6:1-2)

This passage may be overlooked in regard to parents of adult children, but it is applicable because of the authority and responsibility of parents. To honor someone, which means to have weight, to be weighty, is an important concept, it indicates seriousness. The only requirement given for one to honor those in authority over them such as a master, an employer, or a parent is the concept of not to disrespect against a believer. The two words, honor and respect, are not interchangeable, but have different meaning. Honor has the connotation of bearing up under the weight of the concept. Even if a parent or one in authority is cruel, the submissive role still gives honor in order to glorify God. Honor is given to one due to the reputation, position or in reverence. Honor is required no matter the personality of the one to whom honor is demanded.

Respect is terror of the one in authority. Respect comes from fear of punishment or retribution or as the fear of not pleasing another. Respect is earned because of actions. Respect has a choice, honor does not.

God demands children honor parents, therefore, the adult child who abandons or estranges from a parent is in disobedience to the Lord, whether they have just cause for the separation or not. Honor does not demand love or respect. An adult child may not love or respect a parent for the things they did, still they can honor that parent.

This concept of a child's honor to the parent is the concept of honoring God the Father. We may not like what is happening in our life, but we do not curse God instead a Christian continues to honor Him. This concept is learned from honoring a parent even when the adult child is not pleased. The Lord will deal with the failings of the parent. It is never the adult child's responsibility to punish their parent.

A good example is found when David sought to bring the ark of the covenant back to Jerusalem and Uzzah touched it. Scripture says, it angered God and Uzzah was struck dead.

This seems strange since Uzzah was attempting to keep the ark from falling off the cart. David spent three months wondering why it angered God and why God killed Uzzah. The answer came as disobedience. The ark was never to be carried on a cart, it was to be carried with the poles by the Levitical priests. When David saw his disobedience, he repented and then retrieved the ark in the proper manner. (1 Samuel 6:3-11).

The application of this principle in an estranged situation is love. The parent who has been estranged now knows their adult child is in disobedience. The parent needs to stop thinking of a cause, and a solution and start thinking in terms of prayer for the estranged child, fasting and offering intense prayer for their child.

The secular world of psychologists teaches this concept as a parental apology for their misdeeds. In a Christian worldview the parents should apologize for known wrongs. When this is offered the

Christian adult child honors the parent with acceptance of the apology and restoration of the family unit. Even after reconciliation it may take some time to build trust again. Nonetheless, it will be worth the effort for all concerned.

This seldom happens. The example of Cain illustrates the problem when a child will not accept an apology for misdeeds, evil is crouching at their heart's door; the solution is prayer.

In the Sermon on the Mount Jesus addresses this issue. He says,

"You have heard that the ancients were told, You shall not commit murder and whoever commits murder shall be liable to the court. But I say to you that everyone who is angry with his brother, (mother, father, sister) shall be guilty before the court, and whoever says to his brother, 'you good-for-nothing,' shall be guilty before the supreme court; and whoever says, 'you fool,' shall be guilty enough to go into the fiery hell." (Matthew 5:21-22).

Jesus is teaching on Mt. Eremos on the shore of Galilee which formed a natural amphitheater. This sermon began His ministry and He taught on the principles of Grace as opposed to the keeping of the law. He did not abolish the law but came to fulfill it. (Matthew 5:17). He was fully qualified to explain to the common people the true meaning of the commandments God gave in the wilderness wanderings. The first principle in regard to murder explains that anger toward another person is the same as murder.

For the estranged family, this is perfectly understood. The one who has been estranged feels as though they have been murdered and are still walking around but without any breath. The one who does the estranging, feels the loss of their support base and childhood security along with their guilt.

At first the estranger may feel relief they no longer have to be a part of the family, but in time they will begin to squirm under the guilt and the lack of peace. It may show up physically with the inability to sit still, or the constant dissatisfaction at most everything in life. They may quarrel with friends and close relatives still in their circle of contact. Or it may show up in depression and withdrawal from activity. Whichever route it takes the estranger will not feel the pain of the one estranged and will become angrier if that pain is pointed out to them. They will feel the weight of guilt, but most often not be able to identify what is wrong. They may see these affects as a physical ailment rather than a spiritual problem.

One of the key points Jesus is teaching concerns reconciliation. The instructions are clear, don't offer a sacrifice to God if you are at odds with your family. The sacrifice will not be acceptable to God. This is the key verse that leads to the inference that Cain's jealousy of Abel built up. While Abel had a better sacrifice (Hebrews 11:4) Cain's sacrifice was not acceptable due to the condition of his spirit.

The sin of hating one's family or even one member of one's family is an affront to God, because it is adoration of a demon spirit to hate another. It destroys the spirit of the estranger and the emotions of the estranged. Both parties are wounded. The family is the sacrifice to the demon.

The estranged must offer prayer, fasting and forgiveness for the one who has belittled and denigrated them. By the action of the estranged members the one who excluded them may be restored. Until the angry one is restored there will be no acceptance of any of their sacrifice. In essence any ministry attempted by one who has exiled his family will be moot, useless, just noise or busyness.

The serpent wins if he can take a servant of Christ and make them useless in their efforts to proclaim the kingdom of God. He doesn't care how much "ministry" they do. Because the serpent knows, God will not accept the sacrifice of a heart that is angry with another, especially a parent, whom God demanded to be honored.

6
God's Image

GOD'S CHILDREN CARRY His image. When one becomes angry at another, they attack the image of God. Abel died, but was taken up in the arms of the Lord. Abel is part of God's family. Cain is probably part of the vile kingdom of Satan, since scripture says he left the presence of God.

God wanted a family, He put a plan into place to have a family that loved Him as much as He loved them. He gave them all they needed. Even in the punishment of driving them out of the garden was an act of love. It was in their loss and pain they learned about God's redemptive plan to restore His children to a right relationship to Him. Before they ate of the tree of the knowledge of good and evil, they only knew the goodness of God and His provision and love. Now they have succumbed to the twisted deceptions of evil and are aware of its existence. Meaning they are capable of committing evil.

This knowledge of evil entered the world through their disobedience and is passed to every human. Therefore, there is the need for reconciliation to the Father in order for the evil to be abolished in one's life. In His love, God the Father, provided a way for this to happen. The idea of self-esteem and self-image came from humanist psychologists and the Christian word let it sneak into church doctrine by cultural acceptance. This is not the first nor will it be the last secular humanist psychology that will enter into the Christian doctrine. These things are the deceptions of evil that draws one away from the Father in whose image humans are made. When understanding of the Father and His family is understood there is no need for self-esteem because a human's worth is found in the love of the Father.

To illustrate, imagine your child is playing outside and you notice something moving in the grass. As you approach you see a large rattlesnake heading toward the child happily playing in his sand box. You grab the child out of the box and carry him into the house safe from the snake. Then you take a weapon and fight the snake. You don't fight the snake when it has the ability to strike the child. The child is the object of the parent's love, the snake is infringing upon the child's right to life and health. It must be removed so that it cannot injure the child. God removed His children from the sandbox, in order to fight the serpent seeking to devour them. Through the work of Christ on the cross, He gave His children a chance to overcome the deception. Yet, in Genesis 6:5-6 it states God regretted creating man. In Jeremiah 16:2, God instructs Jeremiah not to take a wife or have children.

Why Did God Regret Creating Man?

Because the rebellion in His children was so great, they would not listen to their Father. They heard the lies and deception carefully laid out by the serpent. Man only knew evil at this time. (Genesis 6:5)

Look at Genesis 6:4, Strange huh! The incursion of spiritual beings bringing their realm into the physical realm of man by mating and having children with human women was an attempt to interfere with

God's plan of salvation. God made man to be His children, but the spiritual beings wanted God's children to adore and worship them. The evil plot to infect humankind with evil offspring would prevent the Savior from being born. (Genesis 3:15). The reasoning of the serpent to prevent its own demise. Nonetheless, God's plan will never be hindered or changed either by human or spiritual beings. God found the one man who was not totally infected by evil, Noah. He led him to build an ark to salvage some of the good of God's original creation. (Genesis 1:31)

Love for humans serves no purpose in the plan of evil spiritual beings. The desire of the evil is to create evil beings that cannot be a part of God's family. The diabolical plan to hurt the Father, deny Him a family, and set themselves up as the most high condemns man to eternal damnation. God provided a way to avoid that damnation by putting the wrath toward evil on Jesus. When Jesus rose from the dead, the evil in the world faced defeat. This work of Christ gave a blanket forgiveness to all who would receive it. The key word here is 'receive.' Thus evil works overtime throughout time to hide the way of grace from as many as possible. Family estrangement is a tool of evil to destroy but it also illustrates our separation from the Father.

Or, so the evil beings thought. God will not let go of His children that easy. Instead, God saw one man, Noah, whose heart remained pure in his love for God and honored God with obedience. Even when he didn't understand the plan, Noah honored God and believed he would provide a way of escape for him and his family.

The wrath of God pointed toward those who would seek to deceive His children. The ones attempting to blind them to God's love.

The one's consuming God's children. That wrath came in total destruction of the world through a flood. First God removed His children from the garden to save them from an eternity in the presence of evil with no hope of rescue. Then he removed those hopelessly deceived by evil, so the good would have a chance to thrive. Noah and his three sons start the cycle over with the same commandment given to Adam and Eve. Go forth and multiply. (Genesis 9:1)

Starting Over?

Huh! Does an estranged family destroy the family of origin? That seems to be the indication at this point. There is a lesson from this action. There may be situations that cannot be resolved because the anger and deception have so overtaken the heart, the family unit cannot be reconciled as it was. Forgiveness and honor are possible, but time changes people and the family unit will have a different dynamic after years of disrespect and dishonor.

It was God's broken heart that declared "He was sorry He made man." He couldn't help them. Why? Because God made man in His own image meaning, man had the characteristics of God including freedom. Man had the freedom to choose which God or god he would love and which family he would join. All of mankind except Noah chose the serpent. There was no hope for restitution of the existing family.

How does the estranged family apply this? If there is no hope of restitution of the one who has shut themselves off from the family, they have joined with the other, whatever that other is. There is no need to punish oneself by attempting and hoping the estranged will return.

This doesn't mean hope of reconciliation is lost, it means there is hope in life. If the one who estranged decides to return to the family of origin, they may discover the family no longer exists, parents or sibling's may have passed on, or there is a new family built with other children and the estranged cannot be incorporated into the new family due to contradicting belief systems or lifestyle. Children grow up without knowing their grandparents so they are without a family relationship built in the next generation. There is no cohesive family unit. The one who felt it necessary to separate from their family member, now find themselves in the position of no longer belonging. Sadly, the adult child that estranges from parents, taught their own that children grandparents are disposable and the adult child is now the grandparent, who is disposable. Life moves on and when one is captured by the deception of evil, they will find themselves consumed by the same evil.

When the end of the family unit occurs due to an unresolved estrangement, it doesn't lessen the pain. The family can give renewed hope for a life filled with love and the security of a family unit. This may be accomplished multiple ways. Here are two suggestions;

- An estranged family may find a ministry in helping the homeless who become a part of their spiritual family or
- Helping single parents of small children giving them a new family of grandchildren. The pain of the estranged family becomes a blessing for those who do not have the option of a family.

For the one who left the family, they may do the same. But for some families there is a definite end with no more hope of restoration. It's difficult, but life moves on. God gave Noah the same command He gave Adam and Eve, "Go forth and multiply." For the family that has lost hope of restoration, the command is go forth and multiply by creating another family unit where love, honor and respect dwell. The former family will not be forgotten but the departure of the estranger no longer causes intense pain.

Just as the father in Mark 9 brought his possessed son before Christ and begged for Jesus to banish the evil spirit, so the estranged family brings their loved one to Jesus to restore the right spirit of Christ within them. When Jesus said, "All things are possible with God, do you believe?" The estranged family or family member must be able to say, "Lord, I believe, help my unbelief."

Each person has a different level of belief. As interaction through prayer and Bible study increase so does belief and understanding. Ask the Lord to instill trust in His ability to restore one to a right and fruitful relationship with Christ. By focusing on the heart of the family member reconciliation can take place when the angry one looks upon Jesus and His work to restore God's family.

The hurting, hopeful estranged family/member may approach the Sovereign Lord with an attitude of 'I know God can but will He? And if not, Why not?"

Why Doubt?

Abraham was promised descendants as numerous as the stars or the sands of the sea shore, when he was old and had no children. It looked like a promise that could not be kept. Still, God gave Abraham the miracle of Isaac in his old age. (Romans 4:19, Hebrews 11:12). Jacob and his twelve sons laid the foundation for the nation Israel. Abraham never saw the fulfillment of the promise. Nonetheless, he lived his life in a manner to fulfill the promise.

Even though there is no possible physical human method of fulfilling a need that is supernatural, humans still try. But God says, "Not by might or by power but by my Spirit." (Zechariah 4:6). God shows His mighty spirit in the miracles He gives us. We cannot build anything in our own strength, it will all tumble, but when God builds the house it will stand forever. (Hebrews 3:4 1 Peter 2:5).

> *According to the grace of God which was given to me, like a wise master builder I laid a foundation, and another is building on it. But each man must be careful how he builds on it. For no man can lay a foundation other than the one which is laid, which is Jesus Christ. 1 Corinthians 3:10.*

This passage reveals the major problem causing the estrangement of Christian loving families; a poor foundation. The foundation of the church finds a clever serpent digging tunnels under it which cause a weak foundation to slowly collapse. Often without notice until the building falls in on the inhabitants. Family estrangement of Christian families is one of the serpent's tunnels.

As more families crumble the weak foundation becomes evident, but the problem is so massive the church body feels helpless to fix it. As a result, the church may ignore the cracks and fallacies in the doctrinal foundation for years allowing the serpent to continue to dig and come up from his dark tunnels into the church and bite the members. The serpent is not discerning, it will bite whomever is most available and that availability come from weakness of the spirit which may be sickness, over work, tiredness, stress of finances, or hidden immorality. The physical weakness causes one to forget to care for their spirit. Bible study and prayer often gather dust on the shelf in the corner. This is an open invitation to the serpent. He loves dust and relishes in dirt.

7
The Schemes of the Serpent

THE SERPENT ONLY has one scheme – lies and murder! Because it is clever, the serpent can shape the lies into a believable truth. This section examines the types of schemes used by the serpent upon the vulnerable family member. Most often the estranger is an adult child separating from parent or sibling. Rarely does an earthly parent separate from their child. This is indicative of the Holy Father, who will never leave nor forsake His children. (Deuteronomy 31:8, Hebrews 13:5).

The lies of the serpent laid a clever plotline to the ultimate deception, which is designed to deconstruct the truth of God's word and replace it with the serpent's plan. How do we know an adult child estranging from their parents is a spiritual problem promoted by the serpent?

Jesus told us in Matthew 15:3-9

> *"Jesus replied, And why do you, by your traditions, violate the direct commandments of God? For instance, God says, 'Honor your father and mother' and anyone who speaks disrespectfully of father or mother must be put to death. but you say it is all right for people to say to their parents 'Sorry, I can't help you, for I have vowed to give to God what I would have given to you." In this way,*

> *you say they don't need to honor their parents. And so you cancel the world of God for the sake of your own tradition. You hypocrites!" Mt 15-3-9.*

Jesus is speaking to the Pharisees, which would be the religious leaders. This verse is pointed toward those in the church, not outside. The law allows for an adult child who estranges from their parents to be put to death! That's a shock! So why do Christian adults estrange from their parents and disrespect them? What exactly is the plan of the serpent or the devil?

That question unravels mysticism because there is no plan except to undo God's plan through a slight twisting and distortion of God's eternal family. The serpent cannot create or establish law or physicality. He can only manipulate and deceive. Thus the plan of the serpent is to undo the everlasting, loving family that can be present with God in holiness by destroying the physical picture of an earthy loving human family by estrangement.

Holiness is the key in finding the lies of the serpent. God says repeatedly in the book of Leviticus, "be holy even as I am holy." (Leviticus 11:45, 19:2, 20:26, 21:6 and 8.) This is the book where God is giving the law to Moses and the Levitical priests so they may teach and guide the people in the new land. It takes a month for the law to be given and the angels attend Moses to give interpretation. (Acts 7:53)

> *"Therefore, prepare you minds for action, keep sober in spirit, for your hope completely on the grace to be brought to you at the revelation of Jesus Christ, As obedient children, do not be conformed to the former lusts which were yours in your ignorance but be like the Holy One who called you, be holy. ourselves also in*

all your behavior because it is written 'You shall be holy for I am holy." 1 Peter 1:13-16

Notice the commandment to be as obedient children and be like the Father. God's plan for His family involves the children being obedient to their earthly parents. If the serpent can turn one to disobedience it is for no other purpose than to cause the Father distress. This distress causes the need for discipline (Hebrews 12) God will not leave His children unpunished for deviance and He will not leave them uncorrected in their sin. God's instructions were to teach children diligently, (Deuteronomy 6:7).

Confusion

In a family estrangement there are no good, happy feelings. One party may convince themselves they are better off without their family but there will be a hole and a loss of direction. Family units provide direction and support throughout a lifetime. An estrangement robs the next generations of the knowledge and examples of the former generations. Why then would an adult child want to leave their family of origin?

The strange phenomenon of family estrangement has little research to answer many of the questions. Most of the information comes from family members, mostly parents, that have been estranged. The adult children seldom participate in a study and when they do, they offer little information. It appears the adult child feels the need more than understands a reason to estrange. The most common reasons given include emotional abuse, poor parenting and betrayal which are nebulous and undefinable actions based on perceptions and emotions rather than behavior. The specific reasons based on behavior include:

- Problem with a spouse or significant other
- Interfering in the adult child's finances
- Giving unwanted parenting advise
- The adult child owes large sums of money to the parents
- Aging parents requiring more care
- Substance abuse by either party [30]

This text addresses the loving nurturing family unit. However, in a physically abusive family, the next generation still learns forgiveness and the grace of God in restoration rather than depending upon oneself to heal from gross childhood injury alone. Christ can heal all wounds and when abuse has taken place there is the need for the saving Grace of Jesus Christ to heal both parent and child.

The Christ following family that is estranged loses many of the good things God prepared exclusively for the joy of family members. Again this is the ploy of the serpent, to take from God's children for the proliferation of evil through pride and worship of the serpent. This action assures the individual will not be a part of God's eternal family.

The serpent spoke to the woman with a clever trick. He cast doubt upon God love. This trick is alive and well in modern culture. The Bible is presented as a fairy tale or a book of stories that have no significance on life. "Did God give you all the trees with all this beautiful fruit and then tell you not to eat any of it?"

The woman knows this is not true and she can respond positively to it. However, it sets doubt in her mind and prepares her to question the one she has never doubted.

This occurs with the estranged family. The serpent sets up the first lie and this is the one that confuses the estranged parent because they do not hear the lie and cannot imagine how their child is getting things so wrong.

The estranged adult child will make broad statements and expect the parents to understand what went wrong. Statements such as, "you ruined my life," "you are wicked," "All you care about is yourself." "You have to control everything and everybody." And so on. These statements are designed by the evil one to make the parent doubt themselves. It is interesting that many estranged parents will eventually convince themselves they actually physically abused the child. It doesn't matter which point of view one has in a family estrangement, the statements are lies designed by the serpent to cast doubt on the family unit.

The woman corrected the serpent by saying, "no, we can't eat of the tree in the middle." Often the estranger will defend the family unit in the beginning. But the serpent is just beginning.

"Oh!" the serpent whimpers with a knowing nod and roll of the eyes. He continues his deceitful plot by furthering the doubt in the woman's mind. She knows it is truth they cannot eat of the tree of the knowledge of good and evil, but now she wonders why not? If they are allowed to eat of all the other trees, why not this one which is set prominently in the middle of the garden where maybe they pass by it often. Until this moment, she didn't care, but now she wonders. She looks at this tree in a totally different way. She sees God's command as cruel and selfish.

The lie of the serpent casts doubts on the motive of the parent. It will happen in that moment of weakness or tiredness. Suddenly, the adult child sees the actions of their parents as injustice. This new insight which has been planted in their thinking is expressed by declaring to their parent, "you ruined my life."

The parent feels perplexed at the statement. It addresses the feeling of doubt, not an actual event. The child questions one action of their parent's discipline or teaching as abuse. Following the planting of doubt of the parents love for them, the adult child evaluates their childhood for more 'abusive' deeds of their parents. The serpent sits by and provides commentary on multiple versions of incidents in their life. The child develops a sense of neglect. Mom was always there for brother's football games but not for her banquet. Mom doesn't love her as much as brother. Or, mom pushed certain boy/girl date because she liked them. Mom never cared about the child's feelings toward the date. Now, the serpent has elevated the child's view of mom as a sexual predator. The list of events can go on forever, and for every parent that has been exiled from their adult child's life, they are left to wonder," What did I do?"

The emotional attachment to childhood incidents without proof or other family member collaboration serve as fertile ground for the childhood memory banks of an adult child to expand to events of abuse. To the adult parents these same incidents were necessary disciplinary acts of loving parents. This emotional basis for the estrangement serves as the explanation for the small number of families that are reconciled. The original lies of Satan brought mankind into a permanent state of estrangement from God the Father. For the small number of sinful people that find the narrow gate of truth, there is repentance. The loving parent welcomes the estranged child with open arms in the same manner the father welcomed the prodigal son back into the family. Loving Christian parents are incapable of narcissism because Christ and the Holy Spirit are embodiment of love. Yet this is the most common accusation against Christian parents. A close inspection of the many articles written by estranged children reveal a general state of rebelling against discipline. Again, let me clarify, parents make mistakes, this is not debatable. The problem for the estranged child is the authority of the parents. The estranged child contends the authority was misused. While the accusation may be true, it is also true, it is not the reason for estrangement.[31]

God put His love for His children right into the heart of parents. (Deuteronomy 6:7 and 1 John 4. Isaiah 49:15). How can a parent fight for family reconciliation in the face of such perceived accusations?

Buzz Words

An estranged parent usually experiences the adult child using indefinable statements. The estranger becomes engrained in the buzz words of the 'estrangement movement.' Words have power when meanings are attached to them whether correctly or erroneously. One of the subtle tricks of the evil powers and principalities is to exchange the truth for a lie. (Roman 1:25) This causes worship of the creature (New Age Satanism) rather than the creator. Words and phrases that may be familiar to a Christian ear are used but twisted enough to cause even the strongest Christian to turn New Age Satanism into god and God into the devil. It is a twisted perverse theology, yet it pervades our lives in many ways. One of those ways is through language.

The demon spirit will develop ideas through buzz words repeated until they become a universal description of a family estrangement, no matter the individual circumstances.

Emotional Abuse

Most all parenting skills can be defined as "emotional abuse" if one is inclined to define them that way and the picture painted by the one claiming emotional abuse can be made with many different strokes. The truth may be the 'emotional abuse' is an excuse to explain their own short comings. It is the same with all parenting styles, an adult child can find an excuse for drinking in their 'emotional abuse.' The adult riddled with anxiety can blame it on the 'emotional abuse' of their parents. The problems suffered by adults usually do come from the childhood. People are the result of their childhood. However, it is not the parent's intention to cause the problem with the child but rather to resolve it. Parents discipline to make their children better than themselves. In spite of parenting techniques, choices are individual. One chooses to be a victim and another chooses to learn and grow in knowledge of life obstacles, by overcoming the emotions of discipline.

The book of Revelation speaks about overcomers and their blessings. The fact that Christians are described as overcomers shows there are things to overcome. It will be a different thing for each person.[32] Still the process of overcoming anything remains the same for all, Jesus Christ. Discussion about the acts of parents during childhood can be a step toward healing because the parents can see the adult child's viewpoint and even though they will not be able to relive the adult child's past life, the parents should make amends when possible. The adult child can learn to be a better parent and a better person. If the 'emotional abuse' perceived by the adult child is taken to a parent, then the adult child will have a better relationship with friends and the possibility of family reconciliation.

Railing against family to friends, will soon find those friends avoiding them. Everyone has their own problems they don't need to hear about someone else's. Especially when the rant is given in an angry get even demeanor.

Narcissistic

Almost every person that has estranged from another family member will use this word to explain why they did it. Seldom do they understand what the word implies nor what the culture deems to be the meaning. It is a buzz word that is easily tossed, but difficult to catch.

The Diagnostic and Statistical Manual of Mental Disorders, Fifth Edition also known as the DSM-5 lists symptoms that can be observed and then gives qualifying symptoms to diagnose a mental disorder. It is used by psychologists to determine the mental state of a patient.

Narcissism is considered a mental disorder. Therefore, the adult child calling a parent a narcissist makes the claim their parents are mentally ill and vice-versa.

The DSM lists several symptoms that indicate a person has narcissistic personality disorder or NPD. Some of these symptoms are:

- Sees self as grandiose and expect superior treatment from others.
- Continually demeaning, bullying and belittle others.
- Exploiting another person in order to achieve advancement in life or financial gain.
- Lack of empathy for the negative impact they have on the feelings, wishes and needs of other people
- Fixation on fantasies of power, success, intelligence, attractiveness, etc.
- Self-perception of being unique, superior, and associated with high-status people and institutions
- Need for continual admiration from others
- Sense of entitlement to special treatment and to obedience from others.
- Intense envy of others, and the belief that others are equally envious of them.

This list is used to make a clinical diagnosis along with the clinician's awareness of the person's relationship with friends and family. The person may not be able to function on a social level and have difficulty at work or school. In order for the diagnosis to be held up, the behavior of the person must consistently display behavior that is deviant to cultural norms.

The scripture addresses all of this with much less wordiness, *"Love the Lord with all your heart, soul and mind."* This indicates that one is submissive to a higher power which is trusted and loved. One cannot love the one true God as God and set themselves up as god.

The second part is love others as yourself. Pretty apparent God knew the heart of humans was wicked (Jeremiah 17:9) and in order to overcome the wickedness, they must first love Him in order to follow His statutes and then they would love each other as they carried them out.

The statutes are given by Moses in detail in the book of Deuteronomy as the people are going to live in the land of Israel. God wants His people to succeed and since He created them in His image, He knows them better than they know themselves.

Wait a minute, we are created in God's image and He understands Narcissism? Yes. Because Narcissism exists in the heart of every man.

"there is none good, no not one. But God." Mark 10:18. In Genesis 6:5, *"Then the Lord saw that the wickedness of man was great on the earth, and that every intent of the thoughts of his heart was only evil continually."*

To find out the source of evil that lurks within every human heart look to Genesis 3:5, *'you will be like God."*

There it is folks, that same old lie told in the garden is being told in the church today. When a Christian adult calls their parents narcissistic all they are saying is that their parents are human and so are they. The accusation of calling a person a narcissist is as vile as being a narcissist, because the person is one. It becomes a mental disorder when the boundaries of a loving Savior, Jesus Christ is removed.

Satan has caused the word to be tossed around as if it is a curse word, because it is the spirit of Satan. It is the pride of Satan to call one a narcissist, it is the frailty of man to be one.

Interesting enough that the psychological community has a resource to list the possible causes of narcissism in Gabbard's Treatments of Psychiatric Disorders:

- Excessive admiration that is never balanced with realistic criticism of the child.
- Excessive praise for good behaviors, or excessive criticism for bad behaviors in childhood
- Overindulgence and overvaluation by parents, family, and peers.
- Being praised by adults for perceived exceptional physical appearance or abilities
- Severe emotional abuse in childhood
- Unpredictable or unreliable care-giving by the parents
- Learning the behaviors of psychological manipulations from parents or peers

With the exception of the last three items in the list it appears another term for a narcissist would be entitlement.

When Israel estranges from God and turns to the other gods, they are warned again and again. God's prophet, Jeremiah, is put into stocks, laughed at, put into a well and finally imprisoned. He speaks the truth to them and he is horribly treated. Their reason for treating him this way – because he is emotionally abusing them, telling them that their loving God would let the bad Babylonians do damage to their town or people. After all, they have the temple in their town where God lives, He wouldn't destroy them. Therefore, the people claim Jeremiah is narcissistic and trying to elevate himself at their expense.

The methods of using these terms against another are numerous but the method is still the same. Make the one bad, so the other can be good.

Gaslighting

There is emotional abuse that is clinically recognized and real. This abuse is associated with power imbalance in relationships and can be carried out by bullying a person over looks or personality, or by convincing another person they are not seeing things in reality, even to the point of confusion by manipulating circumstances and environment to convince one of hallucinations. It can be an element of violence and/or torture. (The movie Manchurian Candidate illustrates this technique) It can be expressed by continually making false accusations and extreme defamation.

This occurs as true abuse and is a viable reason for estranging from a family member. However, if this is happening in a Christian family, the one using this technique needs counseling and the peace of Christ in their heart. Honor is shown by the adult child by guiding the parent to resources. If the parent refuses, the child has given honor and is no longer obligated. (Ezekiel 3:20-21)

There are stories of parents turning their adult children in to Child Protective Services and taking them to court as a matter of attempted control and/or vindictive behavior. Or they may be using whatever means available to them to encourage their adult child to talk to them. Only Christ can change the heart.

Toxic

Toxic is another term tossed around in a family estrangement as a reason for leaving a family unit. What does it mean? It is another term that is used for sinful man. Everyone can be classified as toxic at some point or another. We hurt each other and when we are hurt we hurt each other more. This is why marital partners get into arguments. When one gets hurt the other will defend their words or deeds often accusing the other of doing something that caused them to act in such a way. It is addressed in 1 Peter 3:8-9,

> *"to sum up all of you be harmonious, sympathetic, brotherly, kindhearted, and humble in spirit; not returning evil for evil or insult for insult but giving a blessing instead; for you were called for the very purpose that might inherit a blessing." 1 Pet 3:8-9*

One who does not follow this statute will be toxic to his brother, his kin and his fellow workers. Do we not all fall into a category of failure in a relationship at one time or another?

Then what does the estranged family member mean or what accusation are they throwing out when they use the term. It is a term that raises concern. It is a harsh term to describe the treatment of another. When one speaks of a family member as toxic, they will receive sympathy. At the same time the one who is being accused will be maligned whether it is true or not. Soon they will determine either from advise given by friends or their own reading they must separate from this family member in order to have a "decent life" because this "toxic" person ruined their life. It may be years before they realize the harsh judgment cut another loved one out of their life too. Years of meaningful companionship and support are lost.

Anyone wanting to justify leaving a relationship and degrading the other will find a reason in the generic term. But the Bible says, *"do not return evil for evil or insult for insult."* (1 Peter 3:9). When adult children throw these unprovable feelings at their parents, the parents become more bewildered.

No-Contact

The final buzz word can be seen in Exodus 32:7. Moses has gone to the top of Mt. Sinai where God cut tablets of stone, wrote upon them and with the help of the angelic host explained the law to Moses. As Moses worships the Lord and basks in the presence of His God, he receives a mournful message.

> *"Then the Lord spoke to Moses, "Go down at once, for* **your** *(Emphasis by author) people, whom you brought up from the land of Egypt, have corrupted themselves." Exodus 32:7*

Do you see it? God spent time alone with Moses to give him the rules to give to the people so they would be able to live peaceably and within God's righteousness when they entered the land. This occurs three months after they have left Egypt. God is preparing them to go into the land and live as free people for the first time in 400 years. But what did the people do?

There was no trust in their leader. When he was out of sight, the people began to grumble and they begged Aaron to make them a god to lead them out of the wilderness. Three months Moses has led them faithfully behind the cloud of the Spirit in the daytime and the pillar of fire at night. But when Moses takes time to go meet with God and get instructions about the journey the people become restless.

The first question to ask is why did they become so restless after only a few months? This shoulld be enough time to adjust to life in the desert, a few more days shouldn't make that much difference. Especially since a cloud hovered above the mountain to show them God's presence with Moses.

God told Moses to go down because **his** people. At the moment God said 'your', he established a no-contact with them. He didn't want to have anything to do with them. This can be seen more clearly in Exodus 32: 9 and 10,

> *"The Lord said to Moses, I have seen this people, and behold they are an obstinate people. Now then let Me alone, that My anger may burn against them and that I may destroy them and I will make of you a great nation." Exodus 32:9-10*

God revealed His heart. These people whom He raised from Abraham 430 years ago have no regard for Him. They will not recognize God as their God and as the only true God. Instead they return to the familiar gods of Egypt and the characteristics assigned to those gods.

It says in Exodus 32: 8 that once the calf was made, they ate and drank and rose up to play. This concept of play involved gross sexual activity. The practice of homosexuality, group sex, anal and oral sex, pedophilia, violent sex and most any other gross sexual playtime one could imagine. The music played loud, the wine flowed freely, the nakedness of the people undulated as they danced around this calf giving it their perverted worship.

The law which Moses now held in his hands on the stones cut by God and written by the finger of God were already being broken and mocked. The people had no faith in Moses or the God he served who was also the God who rescued them. God has already destroyed mankind once with a flood because of the evilness of their heart, now he threatens to destroy this people, the seed of His nation, Israel, and plant a new seed from Moses.

God is burning with anger. We don't often see a picture of God painted in such a way, but a family estrangement can reveal this anger. A parent that has been scolded and mocked by an adult child and told they are no longer going to have contact with them bears an unbearable pain. When the efforts of the parent to reach the adult child does not reap any benefits, but rather the adult child chooses to denigrate the parent further and make more accusations the parents will find themselves burning with anger. They will say things like "I wish I had never had kids" or" I should have stopped with the first one," or "They will pay an awful price for their deeds." There may be other things a parent will say but these are the most common. Just like God's heart wanted to destroy the family He raised and loved, so does an estranged parent want to destroy their rebellious prodigal child who is serving the golden calf of estrangement.

The Christian family member knows the worship of the world will eventually destroy their family's relationship with the Lord or cause them great grief. The pain is so heavy that erasing the entire population appeared as the best solution to God.

This is not an indictment of God's hating His children, it is an example of the love He holds for them and when they turn away from Him and reject Him, the pain is almost too much to bear so it takes on the form of intense anger. If the children are condemning themselves to separation from God, then God will separate Himself from them.

Estranged families will go through a period when they consider this same deed. It is easier to forget the family member that declares no-contact than it is to attempt to bring them back into the family unit. In fact, an examination of the next verses reveals God's reaction to the gross estrangement and no contact with Him.

Moses saw the disobedience and rebellion and threw the tablets that God gave him to the ground. The people had already broken the laws given on those tablets, in Moses mind they held no value anymore. God gave this nation over to Moses to discipline when He said, "your" people. Moses sees the horribleness of the people's playing and feels the same anger God expressed. He melts the golden calf, grinds it into powder spreading it over the water, then making the people drink it.

This disciplinary action reveals to the people how their worship is seen and what their god is. The gold, a precious metal which represents deity, is put into their bodies for the gastrointestinal system to turn it into dung. (The biblical word for feces) Their god is nothing more than feces.

When Moses turns to Aaron for an explanation, he first blames the people and then says, he threw the gold into the fire and out popped the calf, as if by magic. Moses looked at the people and saw no repentance among those who had worshiped from his disciplinary action. He stands and announces; "all who are with Moses and the God who brought them out of Egypt stand with him and all the sons of Levi stood with Moses." The scripture does not list any of the other eleven tribes. The instructions Moses gave to these men reveal the horribleness of the actions of following after the lusts of gross sexuality as a form of worship.

He said to them,

> *"Thus says the Lord the God of Israel, every man of you put his sword upon his thigh, and go back and forth from gate to gate in the camp, and kill every man his brother, and every man his friend, and every man his neighbor." So the sons of Levi did as Moses instructed and about three thousand men of the people fell that day. (Exodus 32:27-28).*

That little exercise in sexual freedom cost them 3000 men. This left 3000 widows, sonless mothers, fatherless children and absent camp leadership. This was a terrible price to pay for worship of an Egyptian god.

Let's take a closer look at the lessons an estranged family can learn from this incident. (This is not a fairy tale; it is an actual event).

Moses called for those who stood with the Lord. It was a minority. If one stands up against sponsoring a yoga class in the church building, he will most likely be booed and mocked by the majority of the congregation. Few will stand with one who stands up against Satan's' practices.

Moses instructed those men who possessed a sword to start killing the men even their brothers, fathers and friends. This is the ultimate estrangement. The men separated those following the gods of Egypt from those trusting in the God of Israel. Remember they have only been out of Egypt for three months and they have no knowledge of their God other than the deeds of God, which they have seen in the parting of the Red Sea.

While still in Egypt the magicians were able to perform miracles with the "secret arts" as seen in Exodus 7:22 and Exodus 8:7. The Hebrews witnessed five plagues the magicians could not imitate and they saw the works of God in the desert. They still doubted him as the only true God. The making of the golden calf did not denigrate their God, because the Egyptian pantheon included many gods and they felt the golden calf would work beside their God. The death of 3000 men revealed that God does not share His glory with anyone.

> *"I am the Lord; that is My name, I will not give My glory to another, Nor My praise to graven images." Isaiah 42:8.*

Scripture makes it clear that God alone is glorified and there is no syncretism in the worship of God. This was first illustrated by God with the death of 3000 men when His people tried to blend another god into their worship and trust.

There seems to be no innocents in this scenario. It appears all people participated in the worship either actively or passively by condoning it and not stopping it. The passive action is as detrimental as the active. The one who knows better but is passive allows those who are active to be destroyed in their unforgiven state without Christ. This means the passive are guilty of the spiritual deaths of their brothers. Moses interceded for the people. The next verses may leave one scratching their head wondering whether God forgave them or not. Let's look at them.

> *On the next day Moses said to the people, "You have committed a great sin, and now I am going up to the Lord perhaps I can make atonement for your sin." Then Moses returned to the Lord and said, "Alas, this people has committed a great sin, and they have made a god of gold for themselves. But now, if You will, forgive their sin—and if not please blot me out from Your book which You have written!" The Lord said to Moses, "Whoever has sinned against Me, I will blot him out of My book. But go now, lead the people where I told you. Behold, My angel shall go before you; nevertheless in the day when I punish, I will punish them for their sin." Then the Lord smote the people, because of what they did with the calf which Aaron had made. (Exodus 32:30-35).*

We need to remember that God does not change, nor have His statues. (Hebrews 13:8). Therefore, these things written earlier are for our instruction to give us a **hope** in Christ Jesus. (Romans 15:4).

The work of a minister is to intercede for his people. Whatever, the condition of one's family, pray continually for your pastor as he comes before the throne of grace on behalf of his people. This will be exemplified by Bible preaching from the pulpit, humility in the staff with a serving heart and people turning from their sin due to the "foolishness of preaching." (1 Corinthians 1:21).

Moses preached to the people and told them of their sin and their need for atonement. Moses interceded for the people by offering himself as a sacrifice for them. However, Moses did not possess the righteousness which would allow him to be a sacrifice for the people. Still his humbleness impressed the Lord to reveal a bit of His plan to Moses.

"Those who sinned. . . blotted from book." There are those whose hearts remained rebellious and they would continue to spread discontent among the people. They would brag about their life in Egypt and curse God for bringing them into the desert. All this in spite of His provision and loving kindness toward them. Their clothing or shoes never wore out, the critters of the desert were kept from them, they never suffered hunger or thirst and they had tents for shelter. God met all their needs under impossible circumstances. But when they rejected Him, He could not bear the rejection. He sent His angel to guide them while He stayed away from them. He knew His anger could destroy them. He chose to have no contact with the rebellious people, but He assured Moses that all the people would be judged in the future according to their sins. This is the sentence of hope. Not all of those on that three-month journey into rebellion perished. Those whose hearts remained true to God and those who repented will not be blotted out of the book of life.

Stonewalling

Does this mean the estranged family should go 'no contact' with their estranged adult child? No, even though God told Moses He would raise up another race from Moses, He didn't do it. When a family member stonewalls another it is the cruelest form of estrangement. The one leaving the family prohibits contact and this makes any attempt or hope of reconciliation impossible. This action is the physical manifestation of vindictiveness. Its purpose is to punish or get back at the family. It is a form of retaliation and deprivation in the case of preventing grandparents a relationship with grandchildren. The longer the stonewall is erected the less chance of reconciliation, because the one stonewalling enjoys the vengeance they receive from the intense hurt they cause people who love them. The only way stonewalling works is in a loving family. If there is no love there is no pain, there is no vengeance.

In order to counter the pain occurring due to loss, the estranged may seek a relationship with another family that does not have an extended family and be grandparents to children in their church that are long-distance from their biological grandparents or perhaps don't have living grandparents. These techniques come straight from the heart of God. He was ready to build another family. He demonstrated His love for His children and their rebellion causes Him great pain.

He built them a perfect garden, they rebelled. He gave them knowledge to cope outside the garden and one murdered another and turned away from Him. He gave them multiple opportunities to turn to Him for help against the demonic influences, instead they adopted the wicked ways of the demons. God had to destroy them. He kept a remnant of Noah and his family. They were told to populate the earth, instead the descendants of Ham built a tower to heaven to overcome God. He didn't destroy them, He confused their language.

Jacob tricked his father for the birthright of the oldest, then spent years working for his uncle for his wives. The twelve sons of Jacob sold one into slavery. God rescued Joseph in order to rescue the ones who sold him. The Egyptians made them slaves but God raised up Moses to bring them out of slavery. Now while He is preparing them to build their land and prosper they build a golden calf to be their god. God's patience with their rebellion turns to anger against them for their stubbornness.

Moses pleads with God and God relents, punishment is not forgotten merely postponed. Even when an estranged family loves a stranger into their family, the missing piece of the family will still leave an empty hole in the spirit. For the estranged family there are many lessons about the nature of God and the evil in the world that will help those hurting to reconcile with each other and God.

You Ruined My Life

Parents may launch a strong Christian young adult only to experience a disillusioned middle age adult child who blames the parents for teaching them incorrectly or may accuse them of "emotional abuse, narcissism or toxicity." The accusation of one of these is usually expressed in the phrase "You ruined my life."

God knew the heart of His people were cursing Him for their situation in spite of His loving kindness. From a human standpoint, one cannot give love to one who will not receive it. It is the ultimate pain in a relational estrangement. That pain is what God felt when His children turned away and put their love on a dumb golden calf.

What does God do? He drives out their enemies in the land to make a way for them to claim it as their own. They were not strong enough to drive them out on their own, but God would fight their battles with them. The estranged parent removes the enemies from the lives of their adult children through prayer and fasting. But it is God who fights the battle for the family unit to be reconciled.

Reaction to Buzz Words

Turn to fasting and prayer, it works. It may not bring the family back together, because things happen. Death may occur before reconciliation or the estrangement becomes so deeply ingrained in the family unit the interaction cannot be restored even if there is forgiveness. When a family member hears the one estranging from them use these buzz words it calls for prayer, not for confrontation.

Confrontation is desired in the anger. Moses punished in the heat of anger to show the people the depth of their depravity. Still they continued in their rebellion until Moses could only intercede in prayer. A family member influenced or taken in by New Age philosophy can be rescued by the intercession of their loved ones. The benefit of praying for an estranged family member and placing one's hope in Christ is the relief from the intense pain. The missing family member is still missed, but the one who prays for the other will have peace.

The phrase, "It's not about you" screamed at a parent in an out of context setting is the precursor to "no contact." By releasing the planted hatred of the parent into the air, the hate of the parent in the heart becomes a viable excuse for one's own problems. They have officially become the victim and are entitled to their insatiable need for vengeance, which causes bitterness.

The sad part about the scenario is the falsehood of it. Lies are planted in the hearts of the children. Does this mean the children are disobedient? In a way yes, something has happened in that adult child's life that is an act of disobedience to the Lord. Guilt will follow the act but because the act may be politically correct, culturally acceptable, or justifiable in the adult child's mind, they do not take credit for the act of disobedience, but the guilt is heavy and weighing them to a point of breakdown.

This is the point where the parent might be able to diffuse the whole thing, most often with a hug and a word of encouragement. Unless the lies of the serpent already cast doubt on the parent's motives. At this point the evil can convince the adult child the pain of the guilt is the parent's fault. Now the adult child can go full-blown anger at the parent and the explosion releases the guilt building up. However, the guilt is not removed, it is only diffused for a while, thus the child has to continue to attack the parent with a more fierce tirade than before. It becomes like an addiction. In order to have peace, even a false peace, the anger has to find an outlet.

The Problem!

The lies of the serpent are meant to deconstruct God's plan for a loving family in the most destructive manner possible. When a reconciliation is impossible, the serpent celebrates success; leaving an adult child with tremendous guilt when the parent passes. The almost guaranteed result will be the adult child becomes the abused parent by their own children. The adult child often forgets their own children are watching as they belittle and abuse grandma and grandpa. It becomes acceptable to treat old people with distain. All young adult children will become old parents to adult children While they are disrespecting their own parents, their children are watching and learning. The children will have no reason to tolerate any short-coming of their own parent. (Judges 2:10).

> *All that generation also were gathered to their fathers; and there arose another generation after them who did not know the Lord nor yet the work which He had done for Israel. Then the sons of Israel did evil in the sight of the Lord and served the Baals."* Judges 2:10

In only one generation, a Christian family and the knowledge of Christ is lost. Being faithful church attenders mean nothing. The family heritage of faith and His plan for a family is lost. The family has been deconstructed by the lies.

Estrangement of a family is a bold and realistic picture of our estrangement from Christ our Savior due to rebellious sin

8
New Age Influence

THIS CHAPTER REVEALS the incursion of the Baals (New Age Philosophies) in church congregations. Most often without realization it is taking place.

We have been told in Jude 4 that *certain persons have crept in unnoticed those who were long beforehand marked out for this condemnation, ungodly persons who turn the grace of our God into licentiousness and deny our only Master and Lord, Jesus Christ.*

This chapter will reveal those who have slipped in among the congregation. This is not a permission to name names among one's congregation, but it is a warning to be aware of the lies perpetrated among a congregation by congregation members.

This text will address the overview of the invasion and then give specifics. Please stay with the chapter, even if you are in total disagreement, there will be some information that will help one from being deceived by the serpent of old.

It's called New Age. Oh, you say, that's been around forever, ever since the Gnostics. Is this all you got? It's not in our church. This text addresses the family suffering from estrangement, it will provide insight for all Christians and a cause for examination of one's own ministry.

> *ut a man must examine himself, and in so doing he is to eat of the bread and drink of the cup, 1 Corinthians 11:28.*
>
> *Test yourselves to see if you are in the faith; examine yourselves! Or do you not recognize this about yourselves, that Jesus Christ is in you-unless indeed you fail the test? 2 Corinthians 13:5*
>
> *But each one must examine his own work, and then he will have reason for boasting in regard to himself alone, and not in regard to another. Galatians 6:4*
>
> *But examine everything carefully; hold fast to that which is good. 1 Thess. 5:21.*

Even as Bible-believing Christians one must examine themselves frequently in light of many things in order to remain fast in the Word of God and in the trust of Jesus Christ. One must remember the serpent is clever, much more clever than a Christian. This is why the commandment to follow God's word is repeated throughout His book of instructions. It is the only weapon we have against this formidable and clever enemy.

What does this have to do with Christian family estrangement? One may also ask, why does God mention many of things frequently with the specific command to have nothing to do with them at all. To avoid them in all forms.

If God is building a family and this is a major concern for Him with His children, should we not examine why? God knew the dangers of these systems and He knew they would entrap His children, so He constantly gives warnings against it. His strongest warnings come from Deuteronomy when His children are getting ready to enter the promised land.

The gods of the other nations have a spirit of rebellion behind them. This rebellion is against the one and only true God of Isr`ael. Through time the names assigned to the gods may change but the goal of the false religions remains static. New Age is an umbrella title which includes the same gods, whose goal is to attack God's family as it did in the Old Testament. The names have changed but the plot and methods are the same. The children of Israel served the Baals (gods). According to Judges 2:10 they served the gods because the law was not taught in such a way to reveal the ways of God. The next generation lost their history with God and as a result they didn't know God's miraculous rescue of their ancestors. They lost their reverence of God.

Sound familiar? It should. The same method of dissuading a younger generation of Israelites is the same method used to pull a younger generation of Christian children away from their parent's spiritual knowledge and family support. This speaks of the failure of parents to heed Deuteronomy 6:7, *teach them diligently.*

A Barna survey says that a large portion of teens regard the church and the lessons learned as out of touch with their world. Some of the reasons for leaving are:

- The church is fear based, teens often feel Christians demonize everything outside of the church and ignore problems in the 'real' world.
- They express the faith is not necessary for life and the Bible stories taught are shallow.
- Other reasons listed in the survey included hostility toward science thinking Christianity has all the answers without considering science-based industries. In which many want to seek a career.

- The attitude toward sexuality is viewed by young teens as simplistic and judgmental. This leads to a conflict about the nature of Christianity. They don't know the works of God.[33]

Seventy percent of young adults leave the church and their parents belief system by the age of eighteen. A small portion (35%) will return. Barna noted the stated reasons for returning included having families of their own, and having a meaningful Bible study when they were kids.[34]

Loss of meaningful Bible Study serves as the main reason youth raised in a Christian home church environment leave their Christianity behind. This meaningful study is most often conducted in the home with the parents as teachers. In an effort to reach the wayward teens, many churches have moved toward entertaining and social justice rather than Bible knowledge. Entertaining will not hold their heart. No matter how big the church and how fantastic the entertainment, it can't compete with *Harry Potter* or *Disney*. Both of whom promote new age beliefs in their story lines.

Mom's just want to be healthy, so the latest craze of Yoga can be used if you use Christian music and Bible verses instead of the Hindu verses. Right? Yoga comes from the Hindu religion as a means to worship their gods. No matter how much Christian music is played or terminology is changed or church locations are used, it is still worship to Hindu gods. The stretching and holding the body in unnatural positions creates a release of hormones and neurotransmitters which can change the brain chemistry. [35]

The main desire in practicing yoga is to obtain oneness with the universal soul, known as Braham in Hinduism or Nirvana in Buddhism. Every thought, muscle movement, and breath taken during a yoga class is designed to bring a false god into the mind by bringing the participant into the presence of that god. Yoga means "union with god" or "to yoke." By disciplining one's body to hold unnatural poses and to empty the mind through meditation, one can meet with their spirit guide. Once a person has mastered the elements of yoga, their spirit is free to roam around any spiritual realm with their spirit guide. At that point the practitioner believes they have powers of psychic abilities.

No matter how much it is promoted Yoga is dangerous territory to enter because that is the territory of the demonic.

> *Behold you are trusting deceptive words to no avail. Will you steal, murder, and commit adultery and swear falsely, and offer sacrifices to Baal and walk after other gods that you have not known, then come and stand before Me in this house which called by My name and say 'We are delivered!'—that you may do all these abominations? Jeremiah 7:8-10*

It is not possible to worship the other gods in any form and then say because one is Christian that they are delivered from the powers of darkness. These modern gods come in sneaky forms. The representatives of these gods is nothing but when we incorporate those images or representatives into our daily life we are allowing those gods to influence our motives and our thinking. The demons will exacerbate the spirit with yoga, fiction books and shows about witchcraft, following the proclaimed New Age prophets such as Oprah, Deepak Chopra, Russell Brand and a host of other gurus. The family estrangement is not an isolated event but the result of philosophy ingrained in society that promotes self as god rather than dependence upon the one true God.

This concept is seen in Ezekiel 23:37- 49.

> *For they have committed adultery, and blood is on their hands. Thus they have committed adultery with their idols and even caused their sons, whom they bore to Me, to pass through the fire to*

> *them as food. Again, they have done this to Me: they have defiled My sanctuary on the same day and profaned My Sabbaths. For when they had slaughtered their children for their idols, they entered My sanctuary on the same day to profane it; and lo, thus they did within My house. Furthermore, they have even sent for men who come from afar, to whom a messenger was sent, and lo, they come for whom you bathe, painted your eyes and decorated yourselves with ornament; and you sat on a splendid couch with a table arranged before it on which you had set My incense and My oil. The sound of a carefree multitude was with her, and drunkards were brought from the wilderness with men of the common sort. And they put bracelets on the hands or the women and beautiful crowns on their heads. . . Your lewdness will be requited upon you, and you will bear the penalty of worshiping your idols; thus you will know that I am the Lord God. Ezekiel 23:37- 49*

Harsh, isn't it. The worship of self is the foundation of these other gods. The adultery practiced is the recognition of these other gods by serving and worshiping them with our activities of yoga, chakras, entertainment, and abortion. When these gods take root in the heart of a Christian, they bring the honor of self in such things as decoration of the body. It can be expressed by a dedication to cosmetics, tattoos, clothing, home decoration etc. (Please note these things are not gods, they are the manifestation of an idol which allows the gods to influence one's thinking. The idea of self as god) Anything can be made into an idol if it is for the promotion and glorification of self.

In the days of passing their children through the fire, the child (under 2 years of age) would be offered to the priest, who would raise the child as an offering to the demon by placing the child in the burning furnace of the god's image. The mother could not express any grief at the loss of the child or they would lose the financial or cultural gain the sacrifice gave them along with their child. The modern culture offers up abortion. This passage reveals the wicked heart that sacrifices their children in order to gain their own selfish wants. This is the current definition of narcissism that children are using against their parents.

The charges in this passage are against Israel and Judah. The people are worshipping their idols in God's house. Performing yoga on church property is the same thing, it is the worship of Hindu gods in God's house. The slaughter of children is the same as abortion, the painting of the eyes and adorning with jewelry is the same as seduction and the sexualizing of young girls, it includes all forms of sexual immorality. Drunkards brought from the wilderness would be the same as inviting those with no moral standards to be the leaders of a nation or community. The only thing that has changed since the ancient time and modern time is the cross of Christ.

Yet, this is the very thing attacked by the New Age philosophy. Why? Because it is the payment for our penalty. If one rejects the cross of Christ, then they will suffer the penalty of death and torture. The scripture calls it 'terror and plunder." This phrase allows the demonic activity to do as they please with the one practicing worship of them. This could include deep depression, bi-polar anxiety, dissociative personality disorder, gender confusion, disease received from promiscuous activities, nightmares, and haunting. When the demons are given free reign in a person's life, there is no escape and that person will be tormented beyond human comprehension. It is in this terror that some will look for rescue from the only truth, life and way to reconciliation with God – Jesus Christ.

The Church Problem

The preceding chapter revealed yoga to be a problem in the Christian church and among Christian people. A study recently stated that 61% of professing Christians believe in one or more New Age practices.[36] These include horoscopes addressed as astrology in the Bible.

> *And they shall spread them before the sun, and the moon, and all the host of heaven, whom they have loved, and whom they have served, and after whom they have walked, and whom they have sought, and whom they have worshipped. They shall not be gathered, nor be buried; they shall be for dung upon the face of the earth. And death will be chosen rather than life by all that remains of the evil family. Jeremiah 8:2 -3a.*

One may say, "I only read it, I don't worship it". Remember Paul's admonition to the Corinthians. Consider whether life decisions are made by reading a horoscope. It is elevated to a guiding entity. This is the choice of death over life because the continual devotion and following of a horoscope will cause a deafening to the Holy Spirit's direction. It is not taken lightly and it will lead to death of the spirit.

> *And fear not them which kill the body, but are not able to kill the soul; but rather fear him which is able to destroy both soul and body in hell. Matthew 10:28*

It's not only a physical death to which God alludes but rather the death of the soul. In other words, practicing such 'innocent' activities will open a door for the demonic to claim the body and thus kill the soul in hell. Once a demon has been invited into a mind, it is given the right of habitation and that right allows the demon to direct decision making and life choices. In conclusion, reading a horoscope invites a demon into one's thinking which leads to death.

This is serious enough that the body will be disrespected and treated as human feces. This sounds fierce and it is. God has not changed. He is still appalled that those that claim to love Him will practice such vile things. But His love for His children caused Him to provide a way of reconciliation – Jesus and only Jesus.

Abortion is another practice condoned by many church people. It breaks God's heart; His most precious gift of life is thrown into the fire of sacrifice to the other gods. He begs the people in Israel not to do this awful thing. He even says He didn't ask for human sacrifice; in fact, He would not have even thought of it. (Jeremiah 7:31).

The new age belief of reincarnation adds to the abortion dilemma. The main point in the children's card game of Pokémon was reincarnation. The fighting of the characters to the death was not so bad because they could take the character to Jannes and Jambres and have them resurrected.

> *Now as Jannes and Jambres withstood Moses, so do these also resist the truth; men of corrupt minds, reprobate concerning the faith. 2 Timothy 3:8.*

It's not an accident the reincarnation of a child's game has the same 'good' guys which are described as wicked and corrupt in the Bible. This turns the Bible into a book of mean fairy tales and a God who wants to destroy. This belief starts at a young age. By the time that child reaches teenage years, having an abortion isn't so bad, after all, the aborted child may be killed but the child will come back as someone else and probably have a better chance at life. Thus they entertain the thought for justification and support of abortion. It is similar to a child wishing something is true to the point of believing it.

Occultism has entered the church through its membership using Angel boards. Another activity purged of the occult name by calling it angel. The activity is still the same as an Ouija board and will call the same demons giving them the right of occupancy in the mind. The book and movie called, "The Secret" provides a portal to entrap a Christian in smooth sounding words that leads to new age practices. Fiction novels such as "The Shack" lead to a distortion of the three persons of the Trinity.

Many Christians have participated in Christian Labyrinth Meditation prayer. One such practice has been called the Emmaus Road. While it appears to be a great way to connect with Christ it is actually based in ancient mythology and incorporates New Age religious methods of meditation

Contemplative Prayer causes the Christian to believe they can change their circumstances as they would like them to be rather than trusting God with their circumstances. This 'technique' is being taught at women's conferences and local Bible studies. [37]

Christian children in public school are exposed and trained in Pantheism through the celebration activities of earth day. Each one of the practices emulates worship to the god Gaia. Pantheism promotes that god is in all things. Parents are often unaware of the influence these activities have on young minds. The parents are often painted as people who don't care about the children's future because they waste and destroy earth's resources. Children are taught that humans are the cause of all problems on the earth and the only way to restore earth is to limit population and economics.

The New Age promotes a collective consciousness or "the singularity" which is the process of causing all people to think alike and as a collective singularity be able to bring about supernatural miracles. This same idea can be found in Genesis 11 and commonly known as the Tower of Babel.

> *The Lord said, "Behold, they are one people, and they all have the same language. And this is what they began to do, and now nothing which they purpose to do will be impossible for them.*
> *Genesis 11:6*

Churches promote this idea by accepting peoples who worship other gods into the congregation. Speaking truth about the dangers of homosexuality, or the devastation of abortion or denying a yogi to have a class are acts of love not of judgment. The judgement is given when a church does not confront a person drowning in the seductive and hidden worship of another god that seeks to destroy them.

The Golden Rule promotes the Christian ideal, "Do unto others as you would have them do to you." This has been high jacked to be turned into a mantra for all religions "to get along." Christians point to Christ as the only truth. Since Christ is the target of the demonic influence then Christians will be the target of a smear. (John 7:7)

The gift of grace is offered freely to anyone through the blood of Christ who took the death penalty for all. The continual bantering of the new age promotes all religions as a path to God. Therefore, because Christians say Christ is the only way, they cannot be right. The hammer of accusation causes many church congregations to hide the truth they possess and adapt to the world, thus causing them to lose the witness of Christ as the only hope. The church becomes impotent.

For the demonic realm this is true, it doesn't matter what activity, god or goddess is being worshipped as long as it isn't Christ because the demonic realm or foreign gods know, He is the only method of reconciliation of man to God. He is the only path to peace and eternal life in God's family.

New Age-Cause of Estrangement?

The New Age philosophy in all its forms promotes an end-game putting the practitioner in control of one's own life in order to become a contributing member of the collective force. Either way the final outcome is one's own knowledge is their god. It doesn't matter whether the knowledge is true or false if it is a perceived experience which makes it true to the individual causing them to rely upon their own knowledge as truth.

This is the serpent's third lie – "you shall become like gods." It is also an impossibility for one to be god with their own limited knowledge. God repeats the phrase "My people perish for lack of knowledge" throughout the Old Testament along with the warning of turning away from other gods.

> *"Because they hated knowledge and did not choose the fear of the Lord (Proverbs 1:7) they would not accept my counsel, they spurned all my reproof, so they shall eat of the fruit of their own way and be satiated with their own devices. For the waywardness of the naïve will kill them, and the complacency of fools will destroy*

> *them. Bu he who listens to me shall live securely and will be at ease from the dread of evil." Proverbs 1:23-33.*

When an individual lives their life based on their own knowledge they will be an easy audience for a religion that promises enlightenment. This knowledge promised by New Age leads the individual to believe they have a 'spark of divinity' within them that can be reached by attaining enough knowledge. "To enslave people it is easier to do it through the mind."[38]

The problem presents itself in the twisted knowledge the serpent plants into the mind of a willing recipient. Information designed for the sole purpose of deception and enslavement. Knowledge obtained from New Age sources. The only true knowledge comes from the only truth, Jesus Christ. The only way to have a truthful knowledge is through Bible reading and study. The serpent will do all it can to prevent church people from Bible Study. Ignorance of Scripture makes people susceptible to the lies.

When the New Age philosophies slip into a church body the people can be deceived and the serpent can do his work of destroying the family unit. When the serpent destroys the soul of the individual through lies, then the serpent consumes the person. The spirit of the one consumed will break and become immobile (depression, bi-polar, psychosis). At this time the individual is so damaged only prayer from an outside source can bring them to a point of healing. Christian family members will be that outside source for a wounded soul.

This is what happens to one who reaches a point of no contact with their family unit. Whatever ills they perceive happened to them are usually the result of false memories or thinking brought on by the minion driving their life. The longer the estrangement lasts the less likely there will be any chance of reconciliation. As Jesus said in Mark 9, "this kind (demon) only comes out with much prayer and fasting." This is the families weapon against estrangement, then proper teaching may take place in the heart of the one causing the rift in the family unit, bringing about healing of the individuals and possibly the family.

A Christian family experiences the effects of New Age philosophy when family estrangement occurs. Its subtle and powerful influence hides when it twists the truth of scripture. It inflicts shame upon the Christian who challenges the acceptable cultural activity in the church. The entrance into the church family reveals its powerful influence.

The scripture starts with God's estrangement from His children in Genesis 3, when Adam and the woman disobey God's instruction for living in harmony with Him. It took a thousand years before God says "He wishes He had never made man." (Genesis 6:6). This is an expression of His pain from being estranged from His family and His children.

By the time Jeremiah is on the scene, there have been several rescues of God's children by God Himself. He tells the children how to return to Him, but there is continual disobedience.

God's creation had one purpose and that is to build an eternal family. Once this concept is grasped, then the rest of the Bible makes more sense. The serpents purpose is to be like God, (Isaiah 14:13-14). The only way the serpent can have the worship of man is to discredit

God and His plan for man. Satan wants man adoration, God adores His creation of man and wants to be a Father.

Let's return to the small child playing outside in a sand pit. He happily builds his sand castles and totes his sand around. You watch him and smile. Then something appears above the ground level, a split tongue flicks out of the large body of a rattle snake as it coils up close to the child.

A parent will run out to rescue the child, but the snake is ready to strike. The parent knows there is no way the child can be rescued before the serpent strikes. So the parent steps between the serpent and the child, lifts the child to safety and takes the poisonous strike of the snake.

This is what Jesus did. We as God's children are surrounded by serpents ready to strike. Only He can rescue from the pit of serpents. When Christ snatched us out of the pit, He took the strikes. He puts His children in a position of safety. But the child wants to play in the sand and the child sees no danger, so the child returns to the sand where the serpents still abide. They may not strike him immediately because they have already struck the parent. But they will lie silently in wait while their poison reserves rebuild. They will strike again.

We are the child and we return to the pit of serpents. God knows we will be bit so He tells the child, "look at Me." Follow my voice and I will lead you to safety. Jesus has already taken the strike for us. We must recognize his work and stay out of the pit where the snakes reside.

"Look, See how great a love the Father has bestowed on us, that we would be called children of God and such we are for this reason the world does not know us, because it did not know Him." 1 John 3:1

In order to see the great salvation offered, one must see the seriousness of depravity and danger that haunts our every move. What better way for the serpent to hurt the parent it has already bitten than to bite the child they sacrificed their life to save.

New Age religions are a pit of rattle snakes poised to bite and destroy.

9
Contending

IF NEW AGE is the cause of estrangement, how do those beliefs invade a loving Bible-believing family?

After years of striving with His children, there came a point of total rebellion and God confronts His own children. Before this He was the protector, provider and source of Life, but they have so rejected Him, He has no choice except to deal with the children and teach them about the rattlesnakes in the sand pit. He says, "I will contend with you." (Jeremiah 2:9)

It's been 490 years of rebellion. God is patient. So is a parent of an estranged child. They seldom give up hope. Instead, they contend for their child.

What does contend mean? Plead is the word used in the King James Version, other synonyms are to grapple, wrangle, strive, hold a controversy, conduct a legal case. Isn't this the state of the estranged? They want to know why and how to correct the problem. God is asking His children the same questions. *"I gave your fathers everything and the best, I protected them, I loved them."* The reason God refers to the fathers is a method of referring to His history with His children. An estranged parent will refer to the childhood of their children.

The Fight Begins

"But My people have changed their glory for that which does not profit". Jeremiah 2:11

Estranged people share several things such as the depth of pain it causes, the confusion of not knowing why and the exchange of one's loving family for something cheap the world has to offer.

God felt all of these. His people turned away from His loving care for a block of wood. What does an estranged child turn toward? No matter what their reasoning, the root cause of estrangement is exchanging a family for something else. Why would they give it up? God is asking His children the same question.

Remember the devil roams around the earth seeking whom he may devour (1 Peter 5:8), when one is captured by another for whatever reason, the serpents in that person's life infiltrate into the life of the one being captured. If that one is weak, tired, or angry, the serpent will wrap around them and separate them.

The following excerpt comes from a book about New Age philosophy. The author R.T. Daniels opens the book saying he is writing the things the spirit told him during his times of meditation. In other words, these are the direct words of the serpent recorded by one of his human servants.

> *"It is relative easy to control a large number of people. Weapons are not entirely necessary. The first question comes into play for the reasoning for the need to control people. The reason stems from insecurity brought upon by a fragile ego. A powerful individual has no need to control others unless they feel powerless. We aspire*

for what we feel we are lacking. The weakest are actually the one that seeks to control the strong. In order for this to work the weak must convince the strong that they aren't strong in the first place. Therefore, the strong must be convinced to buy into a false reality believing that they themselves are actually weak. The feeling and constant reminder of dominance over others is to soothe the fragile ego of the weak."[89]

King Solomon allowed idols of the other gods to come into the country, but it was the spirit of those idols which captured the imagination and lives of the people by convincing them God was weak and the foreign gods (the serpent) were strong. God gave them 490 years to see the damage and to return to Him. Instead the people allowed the serpent to enslave them.

God tries to remind them of the good He has done for them over the centuries, still they do not listen. In Jeremiah 2:23 – 25 God reminds them of their misdeed. He says, "How can you say, I am not defiled?"

Oh, the heaviness of the statement for the estranged parent. It is a parent's love that drives them to ask the child, "Can you see what that person or action is doing to you, how they are making you a slave to their immoral way of life?" The parent may even continue to describe the immorality of the other just as God did with His children. "Can't you see how he/she is using you for their own pleasure and gain? You seem to have lost all sense in your pursuit of relationship with that scoundrel." Yet, the beloved child scoffs at the parents and says, "I want him/her in my life, I don't want you. Leave me alone."

God wept for His children. They have seen the heavy cost of leaving His protection in their sister Israel (Jeremiah 3:7) and God thinks they will be smart enough to return to His protection of His family. Alas, Judah did the same thing Israel did and rejected God, their Father and turned to the serpent, their enemy.

One of the saddest verses in the Bible follows, "God gave her a writ of divorce." God had to divorce His wife Israel and leave behind His children; the people. However, He will not let go easily. He contended for the love of His children by showing them what they were doing.

An adult child is blinded to the love of the parents and sees only the other, whatever it may be, real or perceived. The mind of the adult child is blinded to truth by the serpent sneaking into the control center of the life, that is the mind, where the emotions and will reside.
The one who has been estranged can hear the breaking in God's voice and see the tears running down His face. They know, they understand His plea. God's family is dear to Him and when He sees His children being deceived by other gods that do not care for them, He weeps in sorrow, because it doesn't have to be that way. God provided a way to bring a rebellious member back into the family. It is a way that does not remove the freewill from the individual but allows them to freely choose the free gift. (Romans 6:23, Ephesians 2:8)

The process can be found in 2 Timothy 2: 13, *"evil men and impostors will proceed from bad to worse, deceiving and being deceived."* The flip side of that verse is found in 2 Timothy 2:14, where Paul tells Timothy, *"You continue in the things you have learned and become convinced of, knowing from whom you have learned them, and from childhood you have known the sacred writings which are able to give you the wisdom that lead to salvation through faith which is in Christ Jesus."*

There is hope for Christian parents, whatever dysfunctional thing happens in a family is not as important as the teachings about Christ from childhood. We know Timothy's family was dysfunctional but we don't know the details. Why? They aren't important. In the same way the dysfunctional part of a Christian family that leads to estrangement doesn't matter.

Support groups and blog groups will focus on the events and accusations. On the other hand, the teachings of scripture from childhood remain in the heart. They are vitally important because this is the way to salvation and a possible restoration of the family unit.

Even if a parent is not reconciled to their rebellious adult child on earth, they will be reconciled with that child in the presence of Jesus and in the light of His beauty nothing on this earth will matter. This is the hope that parents hold. In the book of Jeremiah, it is known as the New Covenant. God says, "I will be their God and they will be My people."

After the work of Christ on the cross and His resurrection there is the indwelling Holy Spirit. It is the New Covenant. God writes His law on hearts of flesh rather than tablets of stone. The Ark of the Covenant contained the stones upon which God wrote the Ten Commandments. Grace writes the law fulfilled in the person of Jesus Christ who dwells in the hearts of believers.

The message stating the ark would not be found is given around 600 B.C. The ark was not present when Rome conquered Jerusalem in 70 A.D. The message says, it will not be missed nor will it come to mind and it will not be made again. No one knows what happened to it and it remains a mystery today. The prophecy is fulfilled. But why would it disappear? Because there is no longer any need of it. When God gives Shepherds after His own heart they will teach God's ways from the Holy Spirit, (1 John 2:27) and God's temple is the heart of his followers.

The message to the estranged parent relates to the future, whether an earthly future or a heavenly future we do not know, but we can infer the earthly family unit can be represented by the ark of the covenant (God's physical place to be with his earthly family) will be transferred to a spiritual plane. The indwelling of the Holy Spirit will bring the family together as God's family. Jeremiah 3:17 says "that at that time when the ark is no longer missed all nations will come to Jerusalem and they will no longer walk in the evil of their heart."

This passage could be referring to the end of the Israelite exile or the end of the present age, or the end of the estrangement. This is because the estrangement will be restored as God intended it to be. This passage shows the healing of estrangement is God's plan.

Jeremiah 3: 21 speaks to the estranged parent. There is weeping because they have forgotten their Lord. An adult child who forgets their parent or is estranged by their parents will have an emptiness in their life, they will have the loss of the support system. The sadness of loss may serve as the stimulus for a repentant heart in the child. But that is God's work, not the work of the parent.

God says to His children, *"Your ways and your deeds have brought these thing to you. This is your evil. How bitter? How it has touched your heart." Jeremiah 4:18.*

Know that as a parent there will most likely not be an apology until the adult child is shunned by their own children. Sadly, that is part of the bitterness of estrangement, it will go to the third and fourth generation, but the blessings of restoration in the family of faith in Christ Jesus will go to 1000 generations.

The Prodigal Child

"But he became angry and was not willing to go in: and his father came out and began pleading with him. Luke 15:28.

This is the brother of the prodigal son, when the father wanted to honor the son who left and squandered his inheritance. The father's answer to the son is found in the following verses when he tells the brother, "you have been with me all this time and all that I have is yours, but now we rejoice because your brother has returned."

This parable is found in the middle of a string of parables Jesus used to answer the Pharisees and scribes in response to their grumblings about Jesus dining with sinners. Jesus tells them "there will be more joy in heaven over one sinner who repents than over ninety-nine righteous persons who need no repentance." This is a look at the application of Jesus words to the Christian estranged family. The parable of the prodigal son is truly an estranged family story.

The young man decides he no longer wants to be a part of the family unit. He takes his inheritance and leaves. This can be compared to the adult child estranging from the family unit. He wants his share of the family holdings but not the discipline. The Father gives the son what he wants and lets him go. This happens in many estranged families. The adult child may drain their parents of finances and then feel the guilt of not being able to pay them back or the estranged family member lives contrary to the family's moral values. It is easier to estrange than it is to face them. But the parable tells the heart of a loving parent will welcome the adult child back with open arms with no mention of the debt or the life they have lived.

At the same time the faithful brother who stayed with the parents becomes angry at the sibling who committed such heinous acts against their parents. This can be a sad outcome in a family unit, when one abuses the parents and the parents forgive but the sibling can't, then the sibling estranges from the brother in anger. We see the father pleading with the son who stayed. The indication is that the faithful son, forgave because his father asked him too. This would indicate the son was raised in the discipline and instruction of the Lord.

Even Christian parents makes mistakes but their strength is in their love for their children. The reconciliation of family may not come in this life, but with both the parents and the adult child seeking the Lord and His ways, there will be joy in heaven when all the prodigals return and forgive their dysfunctional family.

10
The Weeping Prophet

JEREMIAH IS OFTEN called the weeping prophet. God sent His heart to Jeremiah and the tears shed by Jeremiah were the tears shed by God over His people. Let's take a look at Jeremiah 8:18.

> *My sorrow is beyond healing*
> *My heart is faint within me*
> *Behold, listen, the cry of the daughter of my people from a distant land; Is the Lord not in Zion? Is her King not within her?" Why have they provoked Me with their graven images with foreign idols. Harvest is past, summer is ended, and we are not saved. For the brokenness of the daughter of my people I am broken. I mourn, dismay has taken hold of me. Is there no balm in Gilead? Is there no physician there? Why then has not the health of the daughter of my people been restored? Jeremiah 8:18*

Recognizing God's family left Him for other gods, it is easy to see the estrangement of family in these words. "Sorrow beyond healing" is a phrase estranged families use because there is nothing one can do to make it better. While the psychological community will promote techniques to help with the sorrow, they are empty activities with temporary relief from the pain. The answer to why nothing works is in the second line, "My heart is faint within me."

What does faint mean? The Hebrew word is *davvoy* and it means languish, no mental energy, a sickness so deep it causes one to exhaust themselves with no results. It is like the heart melts. This is a perfect description of what an estranged parent feels when their adult child abandons them. Jeremiah 18:22 asks the question, *"Is there no physician?"* The estranged parent wants to find some relief from the weight of the melting heart, but there is no physician that can heal it.

The secular psychology practitioners will give medications to numb the senses or exercises or self-help books, usually books that teach or promote mindfulness or meditation within the New Age belief system.

The next description in Jeremiah 9:1 is the source of the title of weeping prophet, *"Oh, that my head were water and my eyes a fountain of tears, that I might weep day and night."* The estranged parent weeps until there is nothing left. They want to cry more but there are no more tears. One such parent, Sheri McGregor wrote a book called, *Done with the Crying* to help parents heal and move on with life. It has been a help to many.

God wept over His estranged family in the same way. As a Christian family this passage gives comfort. God understands us and we understand Him. His heart, His longing to be with His children is much greater than our own. It draws us to Him in a silent satisfying way like a pet curls up into a bend of the owner's body. It's a place of comfort and safety. It is the place where we find nourishment and healing of the wound.

Paul said in Romans 3, "All have sinned and come short of the glory of God." Neither the estranger nor the estranged are totally right or totally a victim.

Recognizing one's shortcomings on both sides is the first step to healing. An adult child who left will not feel the necessity to mend the rift in the same degree as a parent that has been estranged. This is because the adult child's life moved past dependency on the parents and come to the point of provider for their own family. The adult child establishes their independence and building their family unit. The parents need the child more than the child needs the parents at this stage in life.

Scripture is given for our instruction in order to give us a hope in Christ Jesus. The hope a family seeks is restoration of the family. The prodigal son parable reveals this may not happen until the estranger reaches the end of their resources. How does a family refine the unit so it can be whole again?

God's solution is not a pretty one, nor an easy one. He scattered His people among other nations and sent them into captivity for seventy years. In the next chapter, He fashioned the New Covenant, to provide a way for His children to return to Him.

The estranged family must let them go and rebuild a life without them. It's not easy. It may be the only thing one can do. God's children turned away from Him, so He took the Shekinah glory from the temple and Jerusalem. (Ezekiel 10-11). When the adult child is untouchable and the family cannot bring about restitution, they must let the child go.

The definition of the weeping prophet and the broken heart of God will be seen by the abandoned parent. It shows God's sorrow at the misdeeds of His children that are going to injure the adult child. A Christian parent hears or sees the heart of his bitter child breaking apart with vengeance and knows it will not end with a good outcome. In Jeremiah 9: 10-12, God lays out the poor life situation that has come about because of their estrangement from God. Even nature ceases because of the blight upon the earth. So it is with the family. One member may be estranged from their family, but it will make the joy of the family unit cease. The harshness and deceit cannot be endured by the family. Jeremiah 9:12 asks the question, *who is the wise man that may understand this? And who is he to whom the mouth of the Lord has spoken, that he may declare it? Why is the land ruined, laid waste like a desert so that no one passes through?*

The answer comes in Jeremiah 9:13, *The Lord said, because they have forsaken My law which I set before them, and have not obeyed My voice nor walked according to it. But have walked after the stubbornness of their heart and after the Baals, as their fathers taught them.*

It's not an answer one wants to hear. Scripture interpretation must take place in the culture in which it was written and in consideration of the receiver. In this case God is talking about Judah in the period previous to the Babylonian captivity around 600 B.C. Does this apply to the estrangement problem found in the church in the twenty-first century?

Once understanding comes of the lament of God over His family the same principles can be applied to current situation within the same framework. In this passage, God is asking, who understands this? Estranged families have a difficult time understanding the devastation of their family unit. The estranged family will turn to psychologist, family counselors, pastors, friends anyone who will offer up a possible explanation and solution. The parents are as desperate as if the child is dying from a painful terminal disease.

The next statement is not as clear, "to whom has the Lord spoken that he may declare it?" It may appear God is speaking to Jeremiah, however, the context hints at something else. God is saying, "Who is hearing it so it may be declared?" The question and answer style of the scripture reveals a technique to help the one that is being questioned to find an answer.

Who is hearing? God stated through Moses in the book of Deuteronomy that the people should stay away from the foreign gods. He repeated it numerous times. He gave specifics, stay away from sorcerers, witchcraft, necromancy. Don't follow after the teachings of other gods. Those same gods and enticements were the same ones under the New Age umbrella today. The message from God is still the same. Who is listening? Who will declare it? The answer is hard to bear in Jeremiah 9:14, *"they walk in the stubbornness of their own heart."*

When a society is ingrained with other gods the truth is difficult to hear, even for believers. Jesus address this in John 8:45, *"I tell you the truth but you won't believe Me."* The noise of the culture drowns the gentle words of truth. An estranged family member will hear the rattling and boom of the buzz words used to describe the family unit more often than they hear a sermon or a Bible study.

The New Covenant

The Scripture allows scholars to spend a lifetime researching while at the same time a new Christian or small child will find understanding.

> *The law of the Lord is perfect, restoring the soul; The testimony of the Lord is sure, making wise the simple. Psalm 19:7.*

The Holy Spirit is the teacher for both the scholar and the child. Nonetheless, the reader often misunderstands the concept due to ignorance of the context and culture to which it was written. Jeremiah is written in poetic form and is not in chronological order, often causing the reader to be confused about the message. However, this confusion serves to illustrate the confusion in Jerusalem at the time of the Babylonian seize.

Military seizes most often lasted two years. The invading army would camp outside the city walls and prohibit traffic or goods coming into the city. So essentially they would starve the walled city into submission and surrender. This is happening at the time Jeremiah is writing the words of the New Covenant. He is sitting in the king's prison writing about restoration amid the clamor of the people's intensity for survival. They even bartered their children for food saying, *"today, we eat my son, tomorrow we eat yours."* (Jeremiah 19:9) The desperation level of the city caused the people to lose all human sensibilities. Yet it is in the middle of this chaos that God gives Jeremiah the words of the New Covenant.

As one watches a family unit being pulled apart by poor life choices or ill-chosen words or disobedience to the innate laws of God given to humans as His image bearers, it is the time God is preparing His work to be done. Timing poses a problem for the estranged family. A wounded parent wants the child to return 'now!' But that may not be God's plan because the child and parent are being taught. They are being taught by the Heavenly Father, who has designated them part of His family. Thus the Christian estranged family must trust the Father who promised Malachi 4:6, "the hearts of the fathers will be returned to the children and the hearts of the children will be returned to the fathers."

If there is a prophecy to solve a problem, there must be a problem to solve. The estranged family movement is not new to God. He knew during the time of Jeremiah this would happen. Malachi made this prophecy during the time of Esther, Nehemiah and Ezra. The statement that Elijah will come and bring about the promise places the prophecy in the end times as well as the Babylonian captivity.

The New Covenant performs as the pinnacle of Scripture to connect the Old Testament to the New Testament. It melds history with prophecy, through the person of Jesus Christ.

> *Behold days are coming, declares the Lord, when I will make a new covenant with the house of Israel and with the house of Judah "... this is the covenant which I will make with the house of Israel after those days,' declared the Lord, I will put My law within them and on their heart I will write it, and I will be their God and they shall be My people. Jeremiah 31:31,33*

The Old Covenant-Mosaic Covenant

What is the old covenant? It is often called the Mosaic covenant and was made between God and the Israelites as they came out of Egypt. It is found in Exodus 24. Moses took half the blood of the sacrifice and put it in basins. The other half he sprinkled on the altar. Then he took the book of the covenant and read it in the hearing of the people; and they said, *"All that the Lord has spoken we will do, and we will be obedient!" So Moses took the blood and sprinkled it on the people, and said, Behold the blood of the covenant, which the Lord has made with you in accordance with all these words." Exodus 24:6-8.*

Well, this puts a new light on things. God made a Covenant with the people and Moses wrote it in a book. What was God's part of the contractual agreement called a covenant? He would give them the Law, or instructions how to live in obedience to Him and at peace with each other. The keeping of this law would make one holy and reconcile them to the state of man before sin and separation occurred in the Garden of Eden. The keeping of the law would make one a member of God's family.

Even though the people responded by saying, 'whatever God asks we will do,' they didn't. In fact, the human heart is so deceitful and selfish they couldn't even last until the Law was given. The people broke every moral and pure law while Moses sat in the presence of Angelic beings explaining the law to him on Mt. Sinai.

God's plan for reconciliation with His children progressed in spite of the evil committed by the children. From the moment Adam and Eve disobeyed God to the making and worshipping of the golden calf at Mt. Sinai, God remained patient with His image bearers, wanting that none should perish. (2 Peter 3:9).

God endured with these sinful creatures whom He raised from Abraham to their rescue by Moses from slavery to Egypt. As the Hebrews approach their new home promised to Abraham, (Genesis 13:14-15) they stop, hear God's words from Moses and sincerely believe they will keep the law God will give them; a government allowing all to live peaceably and in agreement. A law that would be kept by obedience. The people would govern themselves. (Like America as a Christian nation following the Bible as the experiment in self-governing) They would not have a king because God would watch over them and would provide leaders who would instruct in the law and interpret it according to their daily life situations. This government is known as a theocracy.

This could be an analogy of a marriage ceremony between God and Israel. God relates his relationship to Israel as a loving husband and calls her His wife. (Isaiah 54:5).

God gave a physical picture of His relationship to Israel from the beginning. She is one with Him.
Genesis 2:24, *"For this reason a man shall leave his father and his mother, and be joined to his wife and they shall become one flesh."* Here in the desert, God reaffirms His covenant with His Beloved. He will guide her, protect her and provide for her. He will be a husband to Israel. All He asks in return is faithfulness through obedience. The newly freed nation of Israel bows and in all humility and honesty take the vow to be faithful to God.

Then comes Mt. Sinai. God is fulfilling His part of the covenant by giving the law to Moses and allowing the angels to explain it to Moses. Galatians 3:19, *Why the Law then? It was added because of transgressions, having been ordained through angels by the agency of a mediator, until the seed would come to whom the promise had been made."*

Paul is relating Jesus as the seed or the promise to Abraham. Why was the Mosaic covenant of the law needed? Because man couldn't keep their part of the Law, but it would reveal the frailty of man and his need for the promise to come. The angels were on Mt. Sinai with Moses and they taught him the law, so he could take it to the Levites and the Levites would teach the people how to live in obedience to God. Paul shows how the Law revealed the need for atonement until Jesus came and revealed Grace through His death on the cross.

God gave the Mosaic covenant so people could see the New Covenant. Without the Old the need for the New would not be seen and if it isn't seen it will not be accepted. As a result, all peoples would be doomed to an eternal separation from God. Because God is Holy and only a holy people can be a part of His family. Holiness is obtained by obeying the law in the Mosaic covenant. But that covenant was broken before Moses came down from receiving it. Man couldn't keep the covenant. Thus the New Covenant which depends only on the strength of an Almighty, Holy and Covenant keeping God had to be ordained in order for God to have an eternal family in His kingdom.

When God gives Judah a writ of divorcement in Jeremiah 3:8 He is relieving them of the covenant. This action not only separated them from the God who rescued them, it allowed God to forget the Covenant too. What did this mean? What was God's part of the covenant? God gave them instruction to become Holy so they could be reconciled to Him as His family. He gave Moses the Law. This was not a set of rules the people were to follow; this was the rules of life to be reconciled to God. Without the Law the people would not survive, they would not prosper and they would not know their God. The laws were communication with the Lord. Since the holiness of God prevented Him from walking among the people as He had done in the Garden of Eden, He had to provide a way for the people to become Holy even as He is Holy so He may walk and commune with them again. When He made this statement He was saying; obey the Law and become Holy so you may live with me as My family. The Mosaic Covenant required blood sacrifices be made along with an atonement sacrifice. It was made once a year by the High Priest with the blood sprinkled on the ark of the covenant kept in the Holy of Holies for the sins of the people.

The crafty serpent knew He could not overcome holiness, but the serpent could cause man to reject holiness by their sinful heart. All the serpent needed to do was keep fooling all mankind to rebel against God, and then they would not be a part of God's kingdom. We know God wants an eternal family to live with Him, but what does the serpent want?

The serpents greatest deceptive gimmick is hiding in plain sight and keeping his work disguised as the work of God. He wants to have the honor that God deserves, but the serpent hates mankind and wants to destroy all humans. Why? Maybe the evil spiritual realm is jealous of the gifts God gives to humans, the earth, procreation and the opportunity for salvation. The spiritual beings have no opportunity for salvation because they have been in Heaven with God and they know Jesus (James 2:19). Still they rejected Him. They have no way to be reconciled with God. They made their decision and Jesus said hell was made for the devil and his angels. Matthew 25:41, *"Depart from Me, accursed ones, into the eternal fire which has been prepared for the devil and his angels."*

God knew the people could not keep the Mosaic Covenant, but it was necessary for them to have it in order to recognize Christ as the free gift of salvation by His death on the cross. By becoming human and teaching God's ways, He then went to the cross and overcame the curse of all mankind, the punishment for all disobedience leading to death. (James 1:15). He overcame the power of the serpent. Hebrews 2:14. Why does the serpent have the power of death? Because in the Garden of Eden, the woman said, "If we eat of the tree in the center of the garden we will surely die." The serpent responded, "You won't die." This was the serpent's second lie on his way to gaining the power of death. The serpent followed his deadly lie with the most devastating deception of all, 'you will become like gods.' Man's greatest path to death is the desire to be his own god.

The New Age umbrella focuses on this lie. It promises 'enlightenment' if one will follow their set of behaviors. These behaviors themselves have no power, but by following them, it allows the serpent and his minions to enter the mind, the life and the spirit of the one believing the lies. Some of the actions called for are:

- mindfulness- focusing on one detail,

- meditation – emptying the mind,
- healings - trusting the serpent, (Chakras)
- astral projection - being god, rising above earthly circumstances,
- mysticism, witchcraft sorcery, necromancy – methods to see the future and talk to the dead and many more lies are used to promise one the ability to be a god.

The problem is, one can only be a god with what they know so the demon spirit promises knowledge of godliness when they are invited into the mind. Once they receive an invitation through any of the above activities and including yoga, they have squatter's rights in that life. The only cure is Jesus, the only one with authority over them, because He alone conquered their power of death, when He rose from the grave after three days.

As the American culture and the Christian church move further away from the Law, the greater influence the demonic world has and the greater the chances of influencing or even capturing the mind of one. The demonic entity will lead his host to do anything that will destroy a family. He turns the murder of abortion into a right of reproduction, he turns the duty of a father to provide and protect a family into masculine toxicity, he turns the beauty of a feminine spirit into the need for equality with men. He makes sexual perversions normal through media, he places pornographic images in front of children and young boys, quickly addicting them, creating a perversion of family relationships. He even uses games to capture a mind, he gives pets the status of human children when one calls themselves the mother or daddy of a dog. They insult themselves and the image of God in them. All of this is for the purpose of destroying the family because it is the earthly picture of God's will. No one is immune.

The only protection against this is prayer and Bible knowledge. The serpent will not be deterred by attending church, sitting in a Sunday school class, attending a women's tea or a men's fishing trip. The serpent is the most active member of any church. Even in the strictest Bible teaching church the serpent looks for a crack and like an earthly serpent squeezes through a miniscule space the demonic creature will do the same. It only takes a crack. The serpent can stretch demonic influence into the mind of a Christian with acceptable invisibility. Once the serpent is fat and the host is unaware, then he brings his vile evil into the life of a Christian, in the form of a broken family.

This is the path leading to estranged families. The infection of false gods into the life of the culture, the church and the individual. The only cure is Jesus.

To Whom Is the New Covenant Given?

In Jeremiah 31:31, the covenant is made between God and the house of Israel and the house of Judah. Jeremiah 31:32 mentions the Mosaic covenant, saying this new covenant will not be like the old covenant. The law was given to Moses on tablets of stone, but this Covenant will write the law on the heart of flesh. (Jeremiah 31:33). It connects the Old Covenant to the New Covenant. God's grace allows the law to become a part of us. It is the innate knowledge of God's ways and expectations of us. It is the Holy Spirit teaching and guiding so that we may have faith to come into the family of God and then to be taught by the law to become a functional member of God's family.

Many times the adult child estranging from their family may not have been taught the law in such a manner to make the family one of honor. No matter what mistakes are made, the Law given to Moses and written on the hearts of God's people by the Holy Spirit specifically says, "honor your father and your mother." There are no conditions, it is a simple command. It is the transition between loving the Lord your God with all your heart and soul and loving each other as self. The first four commandments give instructions on loving God. The fifth demands honor to earthly parents, the picture God gave of His family unit. The next six through ten teaches one how to relate to each other as a family of siblings.

Why is the transition of commandment number five important? Because it connects a Holy God to His unholy family. It is the way that one can find God through family; even an estranged family.

But if the New Covenant was written for Israel and Judah how does it apply to the American culture in the twenty-first century. We find the answer from Paul in Romans 2:13, *"For all who have sinned without the Law will also perish without the Law, and all who have sinned under the Law will be judged by the Law."*

When the Bible uses the word 'all' that is exactly what it means. Therefore, all people sin; some with the Law some without the Law. If Christ fulfilled the Law then He is the Law which is written on the heart of humankind, but not all accept and obey, they will be judged by the Law. "For it is not the hearers of the Law who are just before God, but the doers of the Law will be justified." (Romans 2:13) Those people who obey the Law will be the ones to be included in God's family.

There will be no black sheep, no rebels, no prodigals, no estranged kids in God's family. They will all live under the Law of Christ.

> *"For when Gentiles who do not have the Law do instinctively the things of the Law, these not having the Law, are a law to themselves in that they show the work of the Law written in their hearts, their conscience bearing witness and their thoughts alternately accusing or else defending them on the day when, according to my gospel, God will judge the secrets of men through Christ Jesus." Romans 2:14.*

It may not be evident at first glance but Paul is saying the New Covenant is for all mankind. The only obligation one has to the New Covenant is to accept the covenant as the person of Christ. The Holy Spirit writes the Law on the heart of all people, not just those in Judah and Jerusalem. Those who believe it and by faith accept this innate knowledge of holiness as Christ will be found holy as God is holy and will be a part of the family of God. But those who do not believe through faith that the Law is Christ will condemn themselves because there is no excuse not to know Him. Why? Because God wrote it on hearts of flesh instead of tablets of stone. (Ezekiel 11:10, 2 Corinthians 3:3)

The point is that the Law does not change, even in the New Covenant. What changes is the delivery method. The New Age absconds with that delivery of spiritual hunger and seeking and perverts it so that the person sees a false law and as a result a false god. No one is immune from the deception of the serpent. Only those who have the whole armor of God will be protected from the deception. (Ephesians 6:11)

Paul tells the Israelites the family by faith is built the same way for Jews and Gentiles. (Non-Jews). Paul confirms the Old Testament in Romans 15:8-9. Paul instructs the Jews to watch out for their brothers that are not Jews. When Paul refers to the circumcised he is referring to Jews or Israelites. This comes from the covenant of circumcision that was given to Abraham in Genesis 17. This is the covenant of descendants and a multitude of nations and kings will come from Abraham. The sign of that promise of an unending line of descendants was ratified by Abraham with the action of circumcision. It was the sign of belonging to the family of God. This covenant came from the seat of paternity. The father of the family holds the responsibility of his family and the protection of his household and servants. This covenant is not to be taken lightly for it identifies one as a descendent of Abraham and a member of God's family.

When Paul speaks of the Gentiles (Uncircumcised) giving glory to God because Jesus will come and rule over the Gentiles to give them hope. Without Christ there is no hope, so to extend this covenant to those who come to God through faith in the redeeming work of Christ is a huge thing for people living a useless life.

The words of Jesus recorded by Matthew in chapter twelve addresses the Sabbath to the Pharisees. Again they are trying to trick Him by saying He has broken the law by picking grain for food on the Sabbath. Jesus answers them by quoting the Old Testament prophet

Hosea (6:6) "I desire compassion not sacrifice." This is in response to the picking of the grain as a means to satisfy the hunger of his disciples. Jesus has compassion on His children when they have needs. He addresses the Sabbath by saying *"the Son of Man is Lord of the Sabbath."* The story continues as he heals the hand of a leper and states, *"the man is more important to do good to people that to keep the law of the Sabbath"*. Only the Jewish Pharisees, (these would be similar to lawyers) would be strict about keeping the law at the expense of people. They became infuriated and tried to build a legal case against Jesus. Jesus knew their hearts and the things they were conspiring.

In the same way, a family, especially parents, may not know what event triggers one of their own to estrange, but they can usually sense the bitterness in their heart. We see Jesus pulled away from those who sought to do Him harm. The story reveals that many people watching the events followed Him. This could be applied to one member leaving the family in anger at a parent but the remaining siblings retaining respect and honor for the parents, in spite of the accusations against them.

The passage reveals Jesus healed them all. This is remarkable. He healed all those who followed Him, whether they were Jews or not. In the estranged family, all who follow Christ will be healed, those who are estranged and those who leave the family. It doesn't mean the family will be healed immediately. We see Jesus telling them not to speak of their healing. This seems odd at first, but then He relates the prophecy of Isaiah, *Behold, my servant whom I have chosen; My beloved in whom My soul is well—pleased; I will put My spirit upon Him and He shall proclaim justice to the Gentiles. Isaiah 42:1*

Wow! What a promise! God gave the New Covenant and Jesus is claiming it will be for everyone, not just Judah and Israel, but to all through Himself. Matthew 20-21 quotes more of the Isaiah passage and says, "*Until He leads justice to victory. And in His name the Gentiles will hope!*"

The New Covenant is given through Jesus Christ to all. The spoken words of God through Jeremiah came before Paul became a minister to the Gentiles.[40] This confirms Paul inclusion of the Gentiles in Matthew 12:21, And in His name the Gentiles will hope. Paul quotes this same passage in Romans 15:12. Paul is teaching the obedience of faith to the Israelites and the inclusion of the Gentiles. Paul's mission to the Gentiles to give them a hope in Christ is also a lesson for the Jews to learn this same obedience of faith even though they have the law and the Gentiles don't, yet they came to know the Holy Spirit by the law that was written on their hearts.

Romans 2:14, For when Gentiles who do not have the Law do instinctively the things of the Law, these, not having the Law, are a law to themselves.

The ministry of inclusion of all mankind into the New Covenant is completed in Acts through the ministry of Peter and Paul. The church is established on Pentecost. It was on the date of Pentecost when Moses went to the top of Mt. Sinai to receive the law written on tablets of stone. When he came down and saw the blatant rebellion of God's people against the covenant of the law, he sent the Levites who carried a sword out to slay the people, brothers, uncles, fathers, cousins and friends who had participated in this gross sexual orgy to another god.

The Scripture tells us 3000 people fell to death on that day. When Peter and Paul preached the resurrected Christ and a day of judgement it was Pentecost. The Holy Spirit came in and lighted on the heads of the worshippers. Then the scripture says, 3000 were added to their numbers. This was the beginning of the church and is the actual vision of the New Covenant. It was written on tablets of stone and the people rebelled, it was written on the hearts of His people and people were saved. God is a covenant-keeping God with everlasting lovingkindness. This same God is watching over the obedient estranged family.

Peter gives an orderly explanation of how he knew the New Covenant covered the Gentiles in Acts 11 and it illustrates the working of the church, both then and now. It is worth a read and time to meditate over God's love for all people and His invitation to all to become a part of His family.

Estranged families must continue to invite restoration as much as is possible. When the one who has exiled themselves makes it impossible to have any connection, then their rebellion has rejected the invitation and the rest of the family has the spiritual right to continue without them. God extended His invitation to the Gentile nations, not all have accepted the invitation and those nations will not be included in the eternal heavenly family of God. Christ came as our brother who brought salvation to everyone. (Hebrews 2:14).

Ephesians 3:6, "to be specific, that the Gentiles are fellow heirs and fellow member of the body, and fellow partakers of the promise in Christ Jesus through the gospel.

Interpretation of New Covenant

The writer of the book of Hebrews provides an excellent source of interpretation since he is speaking to the second generation church body. The first church bodies were made up of primarily Jews. The Gentiles were not included until Paul was given a ministry to the Gentiles. Most of his letters address the difference between the Law and Grace while addressing problems arising among the congregations. This differentiation between Law and Grace is still a matter that is often misunderstood and wrongly interpreted. Why? Because the New Covenant is a mystery that is often given a cursory tip of the hat as referring to Christ. Which is not wrong, but how does one make the leap from Israel and Judah to the Gentile church?

The writer of Hebrews continues the connection between the Old (Mosaic) Covenant of the Law written on stone and the New Covenant written on the heart with the indwelling Holy Spirit being the teacher and interpreter.

> *Now the main point in what has been said is this; we have such a high priest, who has taken His seat at the right hand of the throne of the Majesty in the heavens, a minister in the sanctuary and in the true tabernacle, which the Lord pitched, not man.*
> *For every high priest is appointed to offer both gifts and sacrifices; so it is necessary that this high priest also have something to offer. Now if He were on earth, He would not be a priest at all, since there are those who offer the gifts according to the Law; who serve a copy and shadow of the heavenly things, just as Moses was warned by God when he was about to erect the tabernacle; for "See" He says, "That you make all things according to the pattern which was shown you on the mountain." (quote from Exodus 25:40)*

But now He has obtained a more excellent ministry, by as much as He is also the mediator of a better covenant, which has been enacted on better promises. For if that first covenant had been faultless, there would have been no occasion sought for a second. Hebrews 8: 1-7

When He said, 'A New Covenant' He has made the first obsolete. But whatever is becoming obsolete and growing old is ready to disappear. Hebrews 8:13.

The writer of Hebrews is establishing Christ as the mediator of the New Covenant God made in Jeremiah. The function of the Law was to show people how to be Holy so they could be reconciled to God. Even though they broke the Law almost immediately after it was given, God spent years teaching them. Jeremiah 34 – 40 is the account of Jerusalem falling to the Babylonians taking the Jews into captivity. Yet it was at this time, the lowest point in history for Jerusalem that God gave the promise of the New Covenant. God gave Moses instructions to build a tabernacle, a place that God could meet with His people. The instructions were detailed and explicit. Scripture says "God showed Moses the pattern." (Acts 7:44). Even though the New Covenant was not fulfilled until many years later, the heavenly tabernacle already existed. It was the pattern for the coming church.

When Jesus met with His disciples the night before He was taken captive He told them, *"And in the same way He took the cup after they had eaten, saying, this cup which is poured out for you is the new covenant in My blood."* In 1 Corinthians 11:25 it says, *"this cup is the new covenant in My blood; do this, as often as you drink it, in remembrance of Me."*

Then the writer of Hebrews says, *"When He said, 'a new covenant,' He has made the first obsolete. But whatever is becoming obsolete and growing old is ready to disappear."* Hebrews 8:13. In the Sermon on the Mount Jesus said, *"I come to fulfill the Law, not to abolish it."*

Christ's crucifixion abolished the Old Covenant bringing in the New Covenant. After Christ ascended into heaven the Holy Spirit would come. John 14:26.

The Holy Spirit comes to dwell within God's people and He will teach the Law to the heart.
But the Comforter, which is the Holy Ghost, whom the Father will send in my name, He shall teach you all things, and bring all things to your remembrance, whatsoever I said unto you.

The writer describes the tabernacle in the next verses then in Hebrews 9:8 he says,

> *"the Holy Spirit signifying this, that the way into the holy has not yet been disclosed while the outer tabernacle is still standing which is a symbol for the present time. Accordingly, both gifts and sacrifices are offered which cannot make the worshiper perfect in conscience since they relate only to food and drink and various washing, regulations for the body imposed until a time of reformation."* Hebrews 9:8

The writer is speaking of the Old Covenant which required ceremonial washings and blood sacrifice. The activities served as a picture of Christ in the image of the heavenly tabernacle. When Christ appears as the high priest, there is a more perfect tabernacle not made with hands. Hebrews 9:11.

During the time of the tabernacle worship, the high priest prepared himself to enter the holy of holies. After physical and spiritual cleansing, he made atonement for the people. This act gave forgiveness from God for the deeds and words of disobedience they had committed in the last year.

The writer states Jesus is different. He is a high priest, not by heritage but by divine appointment. He came, fulfilled the law, became the sacrifice, became the high priest and became the mediator sitting on the right hand of the Father.

Hebrew 10:20 reveal a remarkable visual of Christ's sacrifice,

"by a new and living way which He inaugurated for us through the veil, that is, His flesh and since we have a great priest over the house of God, let us draw near with a sincere heart in full assurance of faith having our hearts sprinkled clean from an evil conscience and our bodies washed with pure water." Hebrews 10:20

Jesus mediates the New Covenant for all. When the veil of His flesh was torn on the cross, the veil to the Holy of Holies revealed Christ as the Holy of Holies. When Jesus ascended into Heaven, the Holy Spirit came to dwell in the hearts of any person having faith in the promise of the New Covenant and staying faithful to the study of the Law (The Bible) which washes away all our wrong-doings and sins by the blood of Christ through the pure water of the Word of God. (Ephesians 5:26).

Another piece to this puzzle about the New Covenant and how it will be instigated can be seen in the description of the high priest and the rituals of the tabernacle. Hebrews 9:1 states, "Now, even the first covenant had regulations of divine worship and the earthly sanctuary."

In spite of God's pleading, His children didn't return to Him. When he told the King to go and live in Babylon, build houses and plant crops, they rebelled at the suggestion of giving in to their enemies.

God knew there would come a time of punishment for the nations that abused His children. He told Abraham He would judge Egypt because they kept the Hebrews in slavery 400 years (Genesis 15:14.)

The Israelites were forced into captivity in Babylon for seventy years before they were allowed to come back. Sadly, not all came back. Families may find themselves in exile for a period of time and there is opportunity for the family to be restored, but they don't always come back. This could be because the estranged has made a new life for themselves and they don't know how to interact with their family unit. Or it could be a growing apart in beliefs and lifestyle. For example, the child of a farm family moved to a large city and wants to stay in the city even though it is thousands of miles from his family. Some will eagerly return to rebuild and they will face another set of difficulties during the rebuilding process.

The New Covenant gives us an example of how estranged family members should relate to their estranged family member.

11
A Tragic Story, A Happy Ending

GENESIS 37-52 PROVIDES a tragic story of family estrangement. It starts with the favored son of Jacob, Joseph, the son of his beloved Rachel.

Jacob sends Joseph to the fields to check on his ten brothers and take them food and water. The young man approaches his brothers. He often relates his dreams to them. These dreams set him above his family in stature and the arrogant fantasy of the younger brother irritates them.

Joseph didn't do any harm to his brothers physically. He irritated them with his dreams. Joseph spoke of what he knew and what made impressions upon his young mind. Most likely, his dreams were so vivid, and memorable, he wanted to discuss them in order to understand them. But the brothers were tasked with physical labor in the field under the hot son. They didn't have time for intellectual philosophical talks and debates. They probably saw Joseph as the kitchen boy delivering their food. They knew he made reports of their quality of labor back to their father, sometimes the reports were not favorable. Each time he tells them another one of his dreams they become more angry. A plot forms in their minds to dispose of this dreadful braggadocios tattle-tale by killing him and blaming it on an animal attack.

A Tragic Story, A Happy Ending

The oldest brother considers what this will do to their father. He makes a weak attempt to stop the plot. The final consensus is to sell the young brother to a caravan passing through. Joseph is purchased as a commodity to be sold in the slavery market.

The young boy, probably fourteen to sixteen years of age is sold as a slave in Egypt to the head of the prison system. Living in a foreign land he is ignorant of the language and the customs. All alone, separated from his family unit he still works diligently and is trustworthy. As a result, the head jailer brings the boy into his home to be a house servant.

The young man is growing in stature and a pleasing appearance. Soon the jailer's wife makes sexual advances at the young boy. Joseph refuses her. Her anger flares as he runs away from her. She catches his garment to stop him, but he continues to flee away even though he is naked. Alas, he is captured and placed in a prison cell. The jailer's wife claims he raped her. Joseph's master possessed the power to put him to death for the accused crime. Apparently, the master felt some tenderness toward the young man and probably believed he could be innocent of the charges. The jailer places him in a prison cell.

Joseph works and suffers as a common prisoner for years. He helps others escape the rottenness of prison by interpreting their dreams. The prisoners have respect for the young man. He is favored among the prisoners. One prisoner brought a dream to him to interpret. Joseph told him he would be restored to service to the king in three days. The interpretation came to pass. Joseph asked the restored prisoner to plead his case. It is years before his case is brought before the magistrate and Joseph is asked to interpret Pharaoh's dream. At that point the young boy is now a man.

He addresses the governing authority with knowledge of the man's dream. As a result, the king places the young man in control of the countries food supply. He is given a new name and a position second only to the king and the authority to speak for the king.

A great famine comes upon the world and the only source of food is under the authority of the man whom the king appointed, Joseph. In the midst of the famine in an act of desperation, Joseph's brothers are sent to Egypt to obtain food for the family. Joseph recognizes his brothers who sold him into slavery. The family who estranged him now stands in front of him asking his favor. They do not recognize him.

Joseph's spirit rejoices at the sight of his family. Even though they sought to kill him, he wants to reunite. No matter how difficult a situation occurs that causes a family member to estrange from their family, there is a deep desire to be a part of the family.

Joseph asks his brothers to bring their father and youngest brother back with them. He wants to see them all. He will not reveal his identity to them until all the family is present. He has been estranged for 20 years from his home. His emotions are running rampant from joy, to anger, to sorrow at years missed, to gratefulness to see them again.

When an estranged family member seeks to reunite with their family unit or member, the family may flip out on all cylinders. They are bombarded with questions and emotions. Does the estranged still feel the deep-seated hostility toward their family? What if the family does something to make them flee the family again? How do you act after years of silence and estrangement? Joseph felt the same emotions an estranged family feels. He also felt the sorrow of loss of his heritage, time with his family and the years of loneliness in a prison cell.

After some manipulation of the brothers, they bring their father and younger brother. Joseph is so overcome with joy at seeing his estranged family, he has to leave the room so they will not see his weeping. He is speaking a foreign language to them, therefore, they do not know he understands them. He hears details of the family, their fears, their regrets. He leaves the room and weeps at the lost time, that will never be regained.

When Joseph reveals himself to Jacob and his brothers, the brothers gasp in fear, for the young boy they sold into slavery and wanted to kill twenty years earlier, now holds the fate of their family in his hands. They are sure he will have them put to death. After years of estrangement the family dynamics change. Parents grow older and feebler. Children lose identity with family and find themselves clustered with strangers instead of family. Jobs change as well as locations. Life moves on. Joseph's brothers threw him out of the family because they didn't like his personality, often it is with family members that estrange from their family. They may do it because their feelings are hurt or because the family doesn't act in their preconceived ideas. When they attempt to return to their family, it is up to the family to accept their return. The changes in personal growth and circumstances create a new atmosphere and a new family dynamic.

Joseph had the power to punish his family for their misdeeds. Instead he embraces them and says, "what you meant for evil God has turned to good" (Genesis 50:20).

The Rest of the Story

The descendants of Joseph lived in Egypt for the next 400 years. As they multiplied the Pharaoh who didn't know Joseph changed their civil status from citizens to slaves. They remained under the firm and cruel hand of Egyptian slave masters until God raised Moses to bring them out of Egypt.

Moses spent forty years leading the multitude of Israelites back to Israel. That generation and Moses died before they entered the land. The task of claiming the land passed to Joshua, son of Nun. Under his leadership, the land of Israel and the home of the Hebrews was established as God's people.

If Joseph had not been taken a slave, Jacob and his family would have perished from hunger. God used Joseph's estrangement to save the nation Israel. God will use your family estrangement to accomplish His plan. While the estranged family member may never see reconciliation on earth or God's plan, the family learns to trust and pray for those separated from the family. There will be a reunion in Heaven for those who seek the Lord.

The estrangement of Joseph from his family serves as a picture of us estranging from God and leaving his family. Joseph went through many trials and depressions, but there is one phrase that is repeated in regard to Joseph's dilemma, "And the Lord was with him." (Genesis 39:2).

In the same way the Lord is with estranged family members who trust Him, because He knows the pain, the suffering, the need to let out a gut-wrenching cry of agony. He knows! In the end, the outcome was seen.

Estrangement is a spiritual problem and those who trust in the Lord will see His hand turn an awful situation into good. When an estranged family member is in the midst of the estrangement, all they feel is pain much greater than any physical or emotional abuse. It is a hidden pain that destroys the body, the mind and the soul. There is no balm to sooth it, there is no surgery to cure it, there is no medicine to make it bearable, except the one who knows the pain and has the power to bring it about for Good.

Summation

For The Estranged Parent of an Adult Child

- Only the one who estranges from the parent can bring about the reconciliation.
- The estranger probably will not try to reconcile unless the parent offers an apology. Even if there is no hint of wrong-doing in their own view.
- If and when an adult child seeks to reconcile with their parent, the parent may facilitate the healing of the family unit by providing a healthy, productive life for the estranger to return.
- Include a third party in the first contact or to mediate a reconciliation. Allow the one who estranged to select the party. If possible a counselor or mediator would be best.
- Other than building a new healthy lifestyle without that family member, there is little the estranged can do to heal the rift. The one who estranges themselves from the family holds most of the elements of restoration.

In the same way God gave His children faith. It is impossible to please God without faith (Hebrews 11: 6) because that is the only way to reconcile our estrangement from Him.

In truth, there are no sides in a family estrangement, there is only pain. Paul expressed the sufferings on this earth as nothing compared to the glories of our eternal home with our Father when the ultimate family estrangement is reconciled in His Kingdom. (Romans 8:18).

Notes for the Estranged Adult Child

It is the fifth commandment for children to honor their father and mother. This is not a request and it has no extenuating circumstances attached.

If an adult child estranges from their parents, they will:

- Become a hypocrite (Mt 15:7.) The adult child estranging from their parents judge them on a strict level they do not adhere to themselves. Jesus spoke on the sermon on the mount and said if you judge others by your standard you will be judged by that standard. (Matthew 7:1) The only measurement of judging another human is by Christ's standard.

- Withdrawing love from a parent is an insult to God. Jesus taught the greatest commandment of all was to love God with all your heart, mind and soul and the second command is to love your neighbor as yourself. When an adult child withdraws love for a parent, it raises the question of their own love for God.

- Teach your own children that grandparents and parents are disposable. If a parent can be discarded because they have faulty personality traits, the adult child doesn't like, then they are teaching their own children how to discard them.
- If a parent made an abusive mistake and the adult child cannot forgive and overcome it, they doubt God's ability to turn the bad to good. Abandoning a parent does not heal the mistakes, it puts them in a temporary hold.
- Estrangement makes one bitter. The bitterness against a parent is a seed for bitterness against anyone who does not meet the personality criteria. Estrangement over ideas and personality cannot be defined and will only add fuel to one's bitterness, often leaving them alone.
- Estrangement from parents robs one's children of generational information, support and history.
- The adult child estranging from their family loses emotional, physical and sometimes financial support.
- Estrangement from a parent is like spitting on the one person on earth who loves you the most. You may not like what they do or say, but all their actions are motivated by love from God the Father. Parents are the only ones who do that.
- Estrangement hurts one's own personality and well-being. It causes dissatisfaction with life.

The only winning side in a family estrangement is found in the work of Jesus on the cross. This is the place God reconciled His

Summation

estranged family. Can we do any less than trust our Heavenly Father to bring good out of that which is meant for evil?

End Notes

[1] Kylie Agillias, "Difference, Choice, and Punishment: Parental beliefs and Understandings about Adult Child Estrangement", *Australian Social Work*, Vol. 68. No 1, 115-129, 2015 https://dx.doi.org/10.1080/0312407X.2014.927897

[2] Immanuel Kant ethics are found in his observational writings. His writing, "On an Alleged Right to Lie for Philanthropic Reasons,' presents interesting material for discussion. One such discussion can be found, *Russian Studies in Philosophy*, vol.48, No.3 (Winter 2009-10), pp. 26-47 by Abdusalam A. Guseinov, "What Kant Said, or Why Is it Impermissible to Lie for the Sake of Good?

[3] Agllias, Kylie, "Missing family; the adult child's experience of parental estrangement,"*Journal of Social Work Practice*, 2018 vol. 32, No. 1. Pp. 59-72, https://doi.org/10.1080/02650533.2017.1326471

[4] Galatians 3:1-5 is Paul speaking to the church at Galatia. His first words are descriptive of the brain misinterpreting truth. "You foolish Galatians, Who has bewitched you."
The term bewitched is defined in Merriam-Webster dictionary as: To influence or affect especially injuriously by witchcraft, or to cast a spell over.
The word beguile is used in Colossians 2:18 and is translated by the *Commentary Critical and Explanatory on the Whole Bible* as: "Defraud you of your prize," literally, "to adjudge a prize out of hostility away from him who deserves it" [TRENCH]. "To be umpire in a contest to the detriment of one." This *defrauding of their prize* the Colossians would suffer, by letting any self-constituted *arbitrator* or *judge* (that is, false teacher) draw them away from Christ," the righteous Judge" and Awarder of the prize (2 Timothy 4:8; James 1:12; 1 Peter 5:4), to angel-worship.

[5] Butler, Moseley, *Explain Pain*, Adelaide, Australia; NoiGroup Publications (2003)

[6] Moseley, G Lorimer, and Johan W S. Vlaeyen. "Beyond Nociception: the Imprecision Hypothesis of Chronic Pain." *Pain,* vol. 156, no. 1, 2015, pp. 35-8.

[7] Farmers will rotate their crops and allow a piece of land to remain unused for a season. This practice gives the land time to rebuild nutrients and restore the soil to grow nutrition rich food.

[8] Sheri McGregor, *Done With the Crying* by Sheri McGregor to find help with building a life without the estranged family member. This book focuses on parents as the estranged from adult children.

[9] Steven Bancarz, Josh Peck *The Second Coming of the New Age,* (Defender, Crane, Mo, 2018).

[10] Deanna Cooner, *A Gathering of Dragons*, (Stones in Clay Publishing, Newcastle, OK. 2017).

[11] Christine Jarvis, "Becoming a Woman Through Wicca: Witches and Wiccans in Contemporary Teen Fiction." *Children's Literature in Education*; Vol. 39, pp.43-52 (2008).

[12] Interesting to note that referring to a person as a dog was the ultimate insult in scripture, for example Goliath says, " Am I a dog you would send a boy?" (1 Samuel 17:43 "A dog returns to its own vomit as a fool returns to his folly." (Proverbs 26:11) Yet we elevate this same creature to the spiritual level of another human, even regarding the life of a dog more valuable than the life of an unborn infant.

[13] https://momremade.com/estranged-family-stops-talking/

[14] Kristen Carr, Holman, Abetz, Kellas, Vagnoni, "Giving Voice to the Silence of Family Estrangement: Comparing Reasons of Estranged Parents and Adult Children in a Nonmatched Sample." *Journal of Family Communication;* April-June 2015, Vol. 15, Issue 2, Pp 130-140.

[15] Davis, Laura, *I Thought We'd Never Speak Again: The Road from Estrangement to Reconciliation.* New York, NY: Quill. 2002.

[16] Anyone who's reads the Bible knows that neither the Bible nor its characters consider these four personages (God, demons, angels, spirits of dead humans.) equal in attributes (power, character, etc.). There is a huge difference between the attributes of God and the spirit of a dead human being. So why are they all called *elohim*? Because *elohim* is, at its most basic level, a "place of residence" term. That is, if your "proper" realm is some place other than the reality plane **embodied** humans occupy, then you are, by definition, an *elohim*. An *elohim* is a being that is a resident of another, different reality plane. *Elohim* can visit our reality plane and we can visit theirs, at least according to the Bible. There are many occasions where *elohim* (angels, demons) come to earth and interact with humans. There are also occasions where prophets get to see the other "dimension" or reality plane. The most common human path to that reality plane is, of course, death. The "other side" (other reality plane) has its own geography, too (heaven, hell/Hades/Sheol, that sort of thing). https://drmsh.com/the-christian-view-of-aliens-part-4-angels-demons-gods-and-aliens-an-interdimensional-common-ground/

[17] Lisa Takeuchi Cullen," Stretching for Jesus," *Time International*; Vol. 166, Issue September 5, 2005.

[18] *Paul's Letters to a Troubled Church; 1 and 2 Corinthians*, Bob Utley.

[19] the interaction or cooperation of two or more organizations, substances, or other agents to produce a combined effect greater than the sum of their separate effects.

[20] "*Some Southern Baptist leaders are calling on people not to do Yoga, saying the practice is not a Christian activity..*" Associated Press, 2010. Associated Press Video Collection. EBSCO*host*, search.ebscohost.com.

[21] Douglas Groothuis, *Confronting the New Age; How to Resist a Growing Religious Movement*, (Wipt & Stock, Eugene Or.) January 4, 2010.

[22] https://www.thegospelcoalition.org/blogs/erik-raymond/harry-potter-and-christians/ assessed September 2019.

End Notes

[23] Mahoney, Kelli. "Should Christians Be Reading "Harry Potter?"" Learn Religions, Jun. 17, 2019, learnreligions.com/should-christians-be-reading-harry-potter-712316.

[24] Jay Adams, *The Biblical View of Self-Esteem, Self-Love, Self-Image*, Harvest House Publishers, Eugene, Oregon 1986.

[25] J.I. Packer, *Keep in Step with the Spirit*, Old Tappan; Revell, 1984, pg 97.

[26] Candy Gunther Brown, "Christian Yoga: Something New Under the Sun/Son?," *Church History*, Vol. 87 no.3 (September 2018) pp 659-583.

[27] Michael Heiser, *I Dare You Not to Bore Me With The Bible;* Lexham Press, 2015

[28] Michael Heiser, *What Does God Want?*; Blind Spot Press, 2018

[29] https://www.blueletterbible.org/lang/lexicon/lexicon.cfm?Strongs=H6440&t=KJV (assessed September 2019)

[30] Kylie Agllas, "Missing Family: The Adult Child's Experience of Parental Estrangement", *Journal of Social Work Practice*, Vol. 32 No.1, 59-72.

[31] Carr; Ibid

[32] Frank M. Dattilio, "Reuniting Estranged Family Members: A Cognitive-Behavioral-Systemic Perspective," *The Americn Journal of Family Therapy*, Vol. 39. Pg, 88-99, 2011.

[33] https://www.barna.com/research/six-reasons-young-christians-leave-church/

[34] David Kinnaman, *You Lost Me,* Baker Books, Grand Rapids, MN. 2019.

[35] https://yogamedicine.com/how-yoga-changes-your-brain/
Neil Pearson, Neurobiology of Pain, *Yoga Therapy Today*, (Spring 2016)

[36] https://www.pewresearch.org/fact-tank/2018/10/01/new-age-beliefs-common-among-both-religious-and-nonreligious-americans/

[37] If there is disagreement with the statements of Contemplative prayer and Christian labyrinth Meditation, always be a Berean and search for truth in the scriptures. If there is disagreement on an issue, there is cause for concern and searching out scripture with the Holy Spirit as the teacher, 1 John 2:27.

[38] R T Daniels, *The 2nd Renaissance & the Philosophies of the New Age,* Lulu Press, 2015.

[39] R.T. Daniels, The Second Renaissance and the New Age Philosophies, Lulu.com.

[40] Gentile can be defined as anyone of a foreign language or not adhering to worship of true God, a heathen, a pagan. Or gentile is anyone not of Jewish descent.

Don't miss the novel series;
a modern day parable of the book of Jeremiah

Dragon Series

Buster Troye comes face to face with a horrid Dragon. Will he overcome the dreadful beast?

Barbara Troye is lured by her selfish needs into revolt? Can she be rescued from the Dragon's demon?

Dr. Zay Troye sees a Dragon carrying the secret of hell. Can science find the truth?

Rance Troye's wedding is cut short when the Dragon steals the bride. Will Rance's search save her or destroy him?

The pain of Buster Troye's Dragon bite grows from a family division. His final battle is fought by the Dragon warrior.

During World War II, military "Operation High Jump" explores Antarctica and finds the Dragon's lair.

www.StonesInClay.com  www.AlongSideYou.org

Available wherever books are sold.